Jonathan Swift

A Modest Proposal

Edited by
Charles Beaumont
The University of Georgia

The Merrill Literary Casebook Series
Edward P. J. Corbett, Editor

D1468698

Charles E. Merrill Publishing Company
A Bell & Howell Company
Columbus, Ohio

Standard Book Number 675-09441-0

Library of Congress Catalog Number: 70-79858

1 2 3 4 5 6 7 8 9 10 — 73 72 71 70 69

Printed in the United States of America

Foreword

The Charles E. Merrill Literary Casebook Series deals with short literary works, arbitrarily defined here as "works which can be easily read in a single sitting." Accordingly, the series will concentrate on poems, short stories, brief dramas, and literary essays. These casebooks are designed to be used in literature courses or in practical criticism courses where the instructor wants to expose his students to an extensive and intensive study of a single, short work or in composition courses where the instructor wants to expose his students to the discipline of writing a research paper on a literary text.

All of the casebooks in the series follow this format: (1) foreword; (2) general instructions for the writing of a research paper; (3) the editor's Introduction; (4) the text of the literary work; (5) a number of critical articles on the literary work; (6) suggested topics for short papers on the literary work; (7) suggested topics for long (10-15 pages) papers on the literary work; (8) a selective bibliography of additional readings on the literary work. Some of the casebooks, especially those dealing with poetry, may carry an additional section, which contains such features as variant versions of the work, a closely related literary work, comments by the author and his contemporaries on the work.

So that students might simulate first-hand research in library copies of books and bound periodicals, each of the critical articles carries full bibliographical information at the bottom of the first page of the article, and the text of the article carries the actual page-numbers of the original source. A notation like /131/ after a word in the text indicates that *after* that word in the original source the article went over to page 131. All of the text between that number and the next number, /132/, can be taken as occurring on page 131 of the original source.

Edward P.J. Corbett
General Editor

iii

General Instructions
For A Research Paper

If your instructor gives you any specific directions about the format of your research paper that differ from the directions given here, you are, of course, to follow his directions. Otherwise, you can observe these directions with the confidence that they represent fairly standard conventions.

A research paper represents a student's synthesis of his reading in a number of primary and secondary works, with an indication, in footnotes, of the source of quotations used in the paper or of facts cited in paraphrased material. A *primary* source is the text of a work as it issued from the pen of the author or some document contemporary with the work. The following, for instance, would be considered primary sources: a manuscript copy of the work; first editions of the work and any subsequent editions authorized by the writer; a modern scholarly edition of the text; an author's comment about his work in letters, memoirs, diaries, journals, or periodicals; published comments on the work by the author's contemporaries. A *secondary* source would be any interpretation, explication, or evaluation of the work printed, usually several years after the author's death, in critical articles and books, in literary histories, and in biographies of the author. In this casebook, the text of the work, any variant versions of it, any commentary on the work by the author himself or his contemporaries may be considered as primary sources; the editor's Introduction, the articles from journals, and the excerpts from books are to be considered secondary sources. The paper that you eventually write will become a secondary source.

Plagiarism

The cardinal sin in the academic community is plagiarism. The rankest form of plagiarism is the verbatim reproduction of someone else's words without any indication that the passage is a quotation. A lesser but still serious form of plagiarism is to report, in your own words, the fruits of someone else's research without acknowledging the source of your information or interpretation.

You can take this as an inflexible rule: every verbatim quotation in your paper must be either enclosed in quotation marks or single-spaced and inset from the left-hand margin and must be followed by a footnote number. Students who merely change a few words or phrases in a quotation and present the passage as their own work are still guilty of plagiarism. Passages of genuine paraphrase must be footnoted too if the information or idea or interpretation contained in the paraphrase cannot be presumed to be known by ordinary educated people or at least by readers who would be interested in the subject you are writing about.

The penalties for plagiarism are usually very severe. Don't run the risk of a failing grade on the paper or even of a failing grade in the course.

Lead-Ins

Provide a lead-in for all quotations. Failure to do so results in a serious breakdown in coherence. The lead-in should at least name the person who is being quoted. The ideal lead-in, however, is one that not only names the person but indicates the pertinence of the quotation.

Examples:

> (typical lead-in for a single-spaced, inset quotation)

> Irving Babbitt makes this observation about
> Flaubert's attitude toward women:

(typical lead-in for quotation worked into the frame of one's sentence)

> Thus the poet sets out to show how the present
> age, as George Anderson puts it, "negates the
> values of the earlier revolution."[7]

Full Names

The first time you mention anyone in a paper give the full name of the person. Subsequently you may refer to him by his last name.

Examples: First allusion—Ronald S. Crane
Subsequent allusions—Professor Crane,
as Crane says.

Ellipses

Lacunae in a direct quotation are indicated with *three spaced periods*, in addition to whatever punctuation mark was in the text at the point where you truncated the quotation. *Hit the space-bar of your typewriter between each period.* Usually there is no need to put the ellipsis-periods at the beginning or the end of a quotation.

Example: `"The poets were not striving to communicate with their audience; . . . By and large, the Romantics were seeking . . . to express their unique personalities."`[8]

Brackets

Brackets are used to enclose any material interpolated into a direct quotation. The abbreviation *sic,* enclosed in brackets, indicates that the error of spelling, grammar, or fact in a direct quotation has been copied as it was in the source being quoted. If your typewriter does not have special keys for brackets, draw the brackets neatly with a pen.

Examples: `"He [Theodore Baum] maintained that Confucianism [the primary element in Chinese philosophy] aimed at teaching each individual to accept his lot in life."`[12]

                   `"Paul Revear [`<u>sic</u>`] made his historic ride on April 18, 1875 [`<u>sic</u>`]."`[15]

Summary Footnote

A footnote number at the end of a sentence which is not enclosed in quotation marks indicates that only *that* sentence is being documented in the footnote. If you want to indicate that the footnote documents more than one sentence, put a footnote number at the end of the *first* sentence of the paraphrased passage and use some formula like this in the footnote:

[16] `For the information presented in this and the following paragraph, I am indebted to Marvin Magalaner,` <u>Time</u> <u>of</u> <u>Apprenticeship</u>`:` <u>the</u> <u>Fiction</u> <u>of</u> <u>Young</u> <u>James</u> <u>Joyce</u> `(London, 1959), pp. 81-93.`

Citing the Edition

The edition of the author's work being used in a paper should always be cited in the first footnote that documents a quotation from that work. You can obviate the need for subsequent footnotes to that edition by using some formula like this:

⁴ Nathaniel Hawthorne, "Young Goodman Brown," as printed in Young Goodman Brown, ed. Thomas E. Connolly, Charles E. Merrill Literary Casebooks (Columbus, Ohio, 1968), pp. 3-15. This edition will be used throughout the paper, and hereafter all quotations from this book will be documented with a page-number in parentheses at the end of the quotation.

Notetaking

Although all the material you use in your paper may be contained in this casebook, you will find it easier to organize your paper if you work from notes written on 3 x 5 or 4 x 6 cards. Besides, you should get practice in the kind of notetaking you will have to do for other term-papers, when you will have to work from books and articles in, or on loan from, the library.

An ideal note is a self-contained note—one which has all the information you would need if you used anything from that note in your paper. A note will be self-contained if it carries the following information:

(1) The information or quotation *accurately* copied.

(2) Some system for distinguishing direct quotation from para-phrase.

(3) All the bibliographical information necessary for documenting that note—full name of the author, title, volume number (if any), place of publication, publisher, publication date, page numbers.

(4) If a question covered more than one page in the source, the note-card should indicate which part of the quotation occurred on one page and which part occurred on the next page. The easiest way to do this is to put the next page number in paren-theses after the last word on one page and before the first word on the next page.

In short, your note should be so complete that you would never have to go back to the original source to gather any piece of information about that note.

Footnote Forms

The footnote forms used here follow the conventions set forth in the *MLA Style Sheet*, Revised Edition, ed. William Riley Parker, which is now used by more than 100 journals and more than thirty university presses in the United States. Copies of this pamphlet can be purchased for fifty cents from your university bookstore or from the Modern Language Association, 62 Fifth Avenue, New York, N.Y. 10011. If your teacher or your institution prescribes a modified form of this footnoting system, you should, of course, follow that system.

A primary footnote, the form used the first time a source is cited, supplies four pieces of information: (1) author's name, (2) title of the source, (3) publication information, (4) specific location in the source of the information or quotation. A secondary footnote is the shorthand form of documentation after the source has been cited in full the first time.

Your instructor may permit you to put all your footnotes on separate pages at the end of your paper. But he may want to give you practice in putting footnotes at the bottom of the page. Whether the footnotes are put at the end of the paper or at the bottom of the page, they should observe this format of spacing: (1) the first line of each footnote should be indented, usually the same number of spaces as your paragraph indentations; (2) all subsequent lines of the footnote should start at the lefthand margin; (3) there should be single-spacing within each footnote and double-spacing between each footnote.

Example:

[10] Ruth Wallerstein, Richard Crashaw: A Study in Style and Poetic Development, University of Wisconsin Studies in Language and Literature, No. 37 (Madison, 1935), p. 52.

Primary Footnotes

(The form to be used the *first* time a work is cited)

[1] Paull F. Baum, Ten Studies in the Poetry of Matthew Arnold (Durham, N.C., 1958), p. 37.
(book by a single author; p. is the abbreviation of *page*)

[2] René Wellek and Austin Warren, Theory of Literature (New York, 1949), pp. 106-7.
(book by two authors; pp. is the abbreviation of *pages*)

[3] William Hickling Prescott, History of the Reign of Philip the Second, King of Spain, ed. John Foster Kirk (Philadelphia, 1871), II, 47.

(an edited work of more than one volume; *ed.* is the abbreviation for "edited by"; note that whenever a volume number is cited, the abbreviation p. or pp. is *not* used in front of the page number)

[4] John Pick, ed., The Windhover (Columbus, Ohio 1968), p. 4.

(form for quotation from an editor's Introduction—as, for instance, in this casebook series; here *ed.* is the abbreviation for "editor")

[5] A.S.P. Woodhouse, "Nature and Grace in The Faerie Queen," in Elizabethan Poetry: Modern Essays in Criticism, ed. Paul J. Alpers (New York, 1967), pp. 346-7.

(chapter or article from an edited collection)

[6] Morton D. Paley, "Tyger of Wrath," PMLA, LXXXI (December, 1966), 544.

(an article from a periodical; note that because the volume number is cited no p. or pp. precedes the page number; the titles of periodicals are often abbreviated in footnotes but are spelled out in the Bibliography; here, for instance, *PMLA* is the abbreviation for *Publications of the Modern Language Association*)

Secondary Footnotes

(Abbreviated footnote forms to be used after a work has been cited once in full)

[7] Baum, p. 45.

(abbreviated form for work cited in footnote #1; note that the secondary footnote is indented the same number of spaces as the first line of primary footnotes)

[8] Wellek and Warren, pp. 239-40.

(abbreviated form for work cited in footnote #2)

[9] Prescott, II, 239.

(abbreviated form for work cited in footnote #3; because this is a multi-volume work, the volume number must be given in addition to the page number)

[10] Ibid., p. 245.

(refers to the immediately preceding footnote—that is, to page 245 in the second volume of Prescott's history; *ibid.* is the abbre-

viation of the Latin adverb *ibidem* meaning "in the same place";
note that this abbreviation is italicized or underlined and that it is
followed by a period, because it is an abbreviation)

[11] Ibid., III, 103.
(refers to the immediately preceding footnote—that is, to Prescott's work again; there must be added to *ibid.* only what changes
from the preceding footnote; here the volume and page changed;
note that there is no p. before 103, because a volume number was
cited)

[12] Baum, pp. 47-50.
(refers to the same work cited in footnote #7 and ultimately to
the work cited in full in footnote #1)

[13] Paley, p. 547.
(refers to the article cited in footnote #6)

[14] Rebecca P. Parkin, "Mythopoeic Activity in the
Rape of the Lock," ELH, XXI (March, 1954), 32.
(since this article from the *Journal of English Literary History*
has not been previously cited in full, it must be given in full here)

[15] Ibid., pp. 33-4.
(refers to Parkin's article in the immediately preceding footnote)

Bibliography Forms

Note carefully the differences in bibliography forms from footnote
forms: (1) the last name of the author is given first, since bibliography
items are arranged alphabetically according to the surname of the
author (in the case of two or more authors of a work, only the name
of the first author is reversed) ; (2) the first line of each bibliography
item starts at the lefthand margin; subsequent lines are indented; (3)
periods are used instead of commas, and parentheses do not enclose
publication information; (4) the publisher is given in addition to the
place of publication; (5) the first and last pages of articles and chapters
are given; (6) most of the abbreviations used in footnotes are avoided
in the Bibliography.

The items are arranged here alphabetically as they would appear in
the Bibliography of your paper.

Baum, Paull F. Ten Studies in the Poetry of Matthew
   Arnold. Durham, N.C.: University of North
   Carolina Press, 1958.

Paley, Morton D. "Tyger of Wrath," <u>Publications</u> <u>of</u>
    <u>the</u> <u>Modern</u> <u>Language</u> <u>Association</u>, LXXXI (Decem-
    ber, 1966), 540-51.

Parkin, Rebecca P. "Mythopoeic Activity in the <u>Rape</u>
    <u>of</u> <u>the</u> <u>Lock</u>," <u>Journal</u> <u>of</u> <u>English</u> <u>Literary</u>
    <u>History</u>, XXI (March, 1954), 30-8.

Pick, John, editor. <u>The</u> <u>Windhover</u>. Columbus, Ohio:
    Charles E. Merrill Publishing Company, 1968.

Prescott, William Hickling. <u>History</u> <u>of</u> <u>the</u> <u>Reign</u> <u>of</u>
    <u>Philip</u> <u>the</u> <u>Second</u>, <u>King</u> <u>of</u> <u>Spain</u>. Edited by
    John Foster Kirk. 3 volumes. Philadelphia: J.B.
    Lippincott and Company, 1871.

Wellek, René and Austin Warren. <u>Theory</u> <u>of</u> <u>Litera-</u>
    <u>ture</u>. New York: Harcourt, Brace & World, Inc.,
    1949.

Woodhouse, A.S.P. "Nature and Grace in <u>The</u> <u>Faerie</u>
    <u>Queene</u>," in <u>Elizabethan</u> <u>Poetry</u>: <u>Modern</u> <u>Essays</u> <u>in</u>
    <u>Criticism</u>. Edited by Paul J. Alpers. New York:
    Oxford University Press, 1967, pp. 345-79.

*If the form for some work that you are using in your paper is not given
in these samples of footnote and bibliography entries, ask your instructor for advice as to the proper form.*

Contents

Introduction

Jonathan Swift was born in Dublin of English parents in November, 1667, a few months after the death of his father. Godwin Swift, his uncle and guardian, sent him to Kilkenny School (then called 'the Eton of Ireland'). In 1682 he entered Trinity College, Dublin, where he received his bachelor's degree and where he remained until 1688, when the college was closed because of the strife in Ireland attendant upon the enforced exile of James II. At that time Swift went to England and became the secretary of Sir William Temple, a highly respected, retired statesman and essayist.

Swift became a priest in the Church of Ireland (Anglican) in 1695, and served variously as Sir William's secretary and in the Irish Church until 1699, when Sir William died. During these years at Moor Park, Sir William's estate, Swift met his lifelong friend, Miss Esther Johnson, whom he called Stella. Also while at Moor Park, Swift embarked upon such an extensive study in the library there that he might be considered substantially self-educated. The University of Oxford conferred its M.A. degree upon him in 1692.

While at Moor Park, Swift wrote his first major satire, *A Tale of a Tub,* which ostensibly is an attack on errors in learning and in religion. The fictive author is a madman, a hack writer of Grub Street, whom Swift uses to expose pride in false learning, in false theology, in false reasoning. Ultimately he is convicted of the sin of turning his back on God's creation and believing that he, out of himself, can spin a better world. But it is an insane, theory-ridden world, in which his flawed mind can find some little peace. The hack, a passionate believer in all things modern, fails to realize his dependence upon God or upon the accumulated knowledge of the past. In the same volume Swift also published his *The Battle of the Books,* which in allegory continues this battle between the ancients and the moderns, with the ancients winning. Although written before 1700, according to Swift, this volume was published in 1704 and was immediately popular.

After preparing some of the papers of Sir William for publication,

1

Swift in 1700 returned to Ireland, where he remained as a priest for most of the time until his return to England in 1710 as a lobbyist for the Church of Ireland. The next four years were some of the happiest in Swift's life. He became close friends with Robert Harley and Henry St. John, the ruling ministers of Queen Anne's government. The most important accomplishment of this administration was the ending of the long Whig-led war against France, concluded by the Treaty of Utrecht in 1713. During these years Swift helped form the Scriblerus Club, a small circle of wits who declared war upon false taste and false learning and who wrote the satiric *Memoirs of Martinus Scriblerus.* The main members of the club were Swift, Alexander Pope, John Gay, Dr. Arbuthnot, and Robert Harley. Swift wrote the *Examiner,* a brilliantly argued, partisan periodical in support of the Tory government and its efforts to end the war. Other important works of this period in London were the *Journal to Stella,* his letters to Esther Johnson in Dublin, in which Swift with great wit and charm kept Stella informed of the day-to-day events in London; and "An Argument against Abolishing Christianity," a highly ironic essay in which Swift assumes the pose of a nominal Christian who argues for the retention of nominal Christianity. With the fall of the Tory ministry and the death of Queen Anne in 1714, Swift was made the Dean of the Cathedral of St. Patrick's in Dublin. Except for a few trips to England to visit friends, Swift spent the rest of his life in Ireland.

In addition to his conscientious management of episcopal affairs, Swift busied himself with Irish politics and became a national hero with his *Drapier's Letters* (1724). In response to a real danger that the English government would flood the Irish economy with devalued small coins, Swift assumed the role of a Dublin cloth merchant and wrote a series of letters exposing the threat, explaining how to avoid it, and rallying the public spirit of the Irish successfully to defeat the move.

Swift had interrupted his writing of his masterpiece, *Gulliver's Travels,* to write the letters of the drapier. The *Travels* was published in London in 1726. In Gulliver, Swift created an average Englishman whom he set off on a series of four fantastic voyages. In the first voyage Gulliver ends up in a land of pigmies. Swift's satiric method here is, in effect, to place mankind under a microscope as he emphasizes the pettiness of human pride as it shows itself in the pomposity of the little people. In the next voyage, Swift reverses his technique by having Gulliver visit a land of giants, where the grossness of man's nature is exposed. Here it is Gulliver who is the pigmy. In the third voyage Gulliver encounters a series of mad theorists as Swift lays bare man's intellectual pride.

The first two voyages are relatively playful satire on the whole, but the satire of voyage three becomes more probing and bizarre. In the fourth voyage Swift probes the bottom limits of man's nature in the most profound satire in English. He has Gulliver in a land in which the apparently reasonable creatures are horses and the lowest animal resembles man. The horses he calls houyhnhnms and the lowest creatures, yahoos. It is easy enough to perceive that the yahoos stand for man at his most debased, but readers have never been able to agree about what the horses represent. Some critics have suggested that the society of these totally rational benevolent horses is Swift's rationalistic utopia; others that they are deists whom Swift is attacking. Others have pointed out that the horses are in fact flawed and that Swift is exposing how unrealistic and unsatisfactory the life of pure reason is for man who, although capable of reasoning, is also a creature of legitimate human emotion.

As he grew older, Swift suffered increasingly from a disease of the inner ear now diagnosed as Meniere's disease. Much has been written concerning Swift's mental condition in his later years. Added to his senility in his seventh decade, this disease apparently caused such pain that for periods Swift was not lucid. This fact gave birth to the long-held notion that Swift died insane. Most modern authorities now doubt this contention. In 1742 Swift's health necessitated the appointment of guardians for him, and in 1745 he died. Because two of the articles in this present book presuppose the reader's knowledge of Swift's famous epitaph, which he himself wrote, I will end this brief survey of the major events in his life and his major publications by quoting it:

Hic depositum est corpus
Jonathan Swift, S. T. P.
Hujus ecclesiae cathedralis
Decani:
Ubi saeva indignatio
Ulterius cor lacerare nequit.
Abi, viator
Et imitare, si poteris,
Strenuum pro virili libertatis vindicem.

"Here is deposited the corpse of Jonathan Swift, Dean of this Cathedral, where savage indignation can no longer lacerate his heart. Go traveler, and imitate, if you can, his strenuous vindication of man's liberty."

"A Modest Proposal," published in 1729, was Swift's last major satire. Although it is timeless as a work of ironic satire, it is also timely in that it was written at a time and in a place as Swift reacted to a particular situation in Ireland. The modern reader, therefore, might profit by being reminded of the situation which brought forth the finest ironic essay in English.

Since at least the time of Queen Elizabeth I, England had generally considered Ireland an English possession to serve only English interests. In the seventeenth century the wars of Oliver Cromwell laid waste much of the land and many of the churches, and Cromwell rewarded many of his Commonwealth soldiers with grants of Irish lands. One of the strongest oaths yet to be heard in Ireland is "May the curse of Cromwell be upon you!"

Near the end of the seventeenth century the English parliament passed a series of laws which virtually ruined the Irish economy. In 1665 and 1680 the English parliament passed laws protecting the English producers by prohibiting the exporting from Ireland into England of all cattle, swine, sheep, and the edible products thereof. In 1663 the Navigation Act of 1660 was amended to exclude Ireland from almost all of the rich trade with the English colonies. The English parliament in 1669 prohibited the colonies of England from shipping directly to Ireland; these goods had to sail in English ships to English ports first. Irish products not specifically banned from England were often in effect prohibited by excessive excise taxes, sometimes as high as 30 per cent. Ireland could still trade with most of the continental powers, but England and the English colonies were the natural direction for Irish trade.

In 1699 the English parliament passed an extremely severe bill prohibiting the exportation of Irish wool in any form to any country in the world. Thus in one stroke the substantial and growing Irish woolen industry was destroyed to protect English woolens. Of all Irish industry only her then small linen and flax crafts did not compete seriously with their English counterparts and were allowed to thrive.

England, in essence, treated Ireland as a colony, as a "depending Kingdom," to use Swift's phrase. In his *Drapier's Letters* and elsewhere Swift argued that Ireland was not a dependent possession of England, but rather one of the equal sister kingdoms of the united kingdoms of England, Ireland, and Scotland. As such, Ireland was an independent kingdom with an independent parliament joined to

England only by the crown: two otherwise independent kingdoms sharing the same monarch. Swift wanted for Ireland what the Act of Union in the reign of Queen Anne had gained for Scotland. (This goal of Swift's was not achieved by Ireland until January 1, 1801, and Swift's patriotic Irish tracts surely helped rally the Irish to reach this goal, which was destroyed by the final Irish revolution of 1916-1924.)

In addition to this crippling of Irish trade, Ireland suffered from the economic abuses of absentee landlords. Since before the time of Elizabeth I, Irish titles and estates and royal appointments were part of English Court patronage and given almost exclusively to Englishmen who lived mostly out of Ireland and who thus spent most of their Irish revenues outside of that kingdom, thus causing a perpetual drain on the Irish economy. In a letter to Alexander Pope, Swift estimated this drain to be two-thirds of all Irish revenues. Added to this general historical background for Swift's great essay is the fact that during the three years preceding the publication of "A Modest Proposal" Ireland had suffered near famine with the failure of the grain crops. Near the end of "An Answer to the *Craftsman*" Swift asserts that Irishmen, to preserve their few cattle, were forced to bleed the cattle and drink that nutritive blood mixed with clabber. Into this seemingly hopeless situation stepped Dean Swift, once again as Irish patriot and master ironist, with his "A Modest Proposal," pushing to the ultimate logical extreme the basic English assumptions governing her treatment of Ireland.

Generically defined, *irony* is the difference between what actually is true and what a person either thinks or pretends to think is true. It is a contrast, often painful, between the real and the illusory. As is usual with him, Swift creates a fictive author (a *persona*, a mask) to be his spokesman. Since his name is not given, most readers call him simply the Modest Proposer. One of Swift's standard ironic devices is to use his opponent in such an argument as the model for his *persona* and then to expose the opponent's position as the character and mind and values of that *persona* are gradually revealed to the audience. This is Swift's tactic in this essay. Thus Swift sets up a powerful irony based upon the contrast between the inhuman proposal which the Modest Proposer sets forth as a good solution for the ills of Ireland and the implied, compassionate solution which the reader is asked to supply. A reader might, for example, adduce that Swift favors an Ireland who can properly nurture her children without material want. Or a reader might adduce that Swift favors no more than a political settlement described in paragraph two, above. In adopting such an unrelenting ironic attack, Swift has made his thrusts mainly negative. By ironically arguing for the wrong solution for the wrong reasons, Swift scarcely leaves himself room for a positive statement. The nearest he comes to a positive exposition of his ideas is in the long, italicized passage near the end of his essay. Otherwise, the reader is left to do much of the work as he ferrets his way through the irony.

The Modest Proposer is extremely and foolishly pro-British. His proposal is simply a better way to accomplish what the English parliament seems intent upon. Naively, he examines the effect of English laws on Ireland and deduces that their ultimate purpose is to cause the deaths of Irishmen (since that is in fact what they are causing). Because the English laws cause these effects, the proposer does not for a moment question such laws: they must be right, for it is unthinkable that the English parliament in its great wisdom would ever pass a law, the full implications of which it did not foresee. The Modest Proposer simply offers a more profitable method of accomplishing the same thing: the desired deaths of Irishmen can turn an additional profit to Ireland, which in turn will make Ireland a richer plum for the English. This is the ironic axis of Swift's essay; Swift pretends and has his Proposer believe that the intended aim and the actual results of these English laws are the death of the Irish. For an irony to be successful, it must contain a kernel of truth. These English laws must, as in fact they did, have a generally disastrous effect on Ireland. Then Swift as satiric ironist can use the exaggeration proper for an ironist and reduce the general situation to its logical extreme. No amount of satiric and ironic art would have been sufficient for Swift to have written a similar satire on England's economic strangulation of Japan because there would have been no truth from which to work and to build the ironic exaggeration upon. The audience must be able to spot this truth in order to follow the ironic extension and exaggeration of it in much the same way that a caricature in the cartoon on the editorial page of our morning newspaper must be a caricature of *some*body: it must contain the recognizable truth of the person even though the artist has exaggerated for satiric effect. Such freedom of exaggeration allows the ironist to refocus the data so that the audience can perceive the data in a new combination and perhaps thus perceive the essential truth of the situation.

Swift's sheer artistry of satiric irony in "A Modest Proposal" makes it enduringly appealing to successive generations of readers, not for the specifics of English policy in Ireland in the first quarter of the eighteenth century — although these specifics (the truths upon which the irony is based) certainly must be known as background for a reader's full appreciation of Swift's essay. But it is the art of Swift which continues to attract and to which the user of this casebook should give his main attention.

Although neither Swift nor anyone else has ever surpassed the art of "A Modest Proposal," Swift did return to the general subject and technique of this essay in its sequel, "An Answer to the *Craftsman*," which is printed here because it is an interesting and important sequel and because it offers the reader an excellent means of studying Swift's techniques in a second and related essay.

In 1730, the year following the publication of "A Modest Proposal," several French army officers, under permission granted by the English crown, began recruiting Irishmen for the armies of the French king, who so late had been England's enemy and who was to be again in the not very distant future. Swift disapproved of the granting of such permission, as did some of the Irish Whig apologists for the English policy. The Tory newspaper, the *Craftsman*, printed an ably written and well argued essay disapproving of the use of Irish troops in the French army and especially of the English government's making such recruitment so easy for the French and the Irish. The author of this essay points out that, alarming as the number of such Irish troops is, the French system of maintaining them in separate Irish regiments is an even graver threat to the Protestant Succession on the English throne because these Roman Catholic English subjects in the pay of the French king and the Pretender could serve to encourage rebellion in England and Ireland in a way that foreigners could not. He also points out that, in addition to the Irish officers of these regiments, the noncommissioned officers form a well-trained cadre which could quickly be expanded into a staff of field-grade officers for rapid enlargement of these Irish regiments into well-staffed armies. He states that the procedure is patently illegal, for the Irish Code makes it a felony for any subject to enlist or to cause others to enlist in the service of any foreign prince. Furthermore, if the English king this one time allows the raising of French troops in Ireland, how will the Irish illiterates know in the future whether they sign up with frauds who merely pretend to have the English king's permission? If the English king grants this permission to the French king, it is likely that his "Catholick Majesty" of Spain might demand equal rights and thus make refusal a pretense for war to capture Gibraltar. The sad state of the Irish economy has already forced many of her people to emigrate, and she can hardly afford this further drain upon her population. This license, he continues, would encourage the Irish to continue to be Roman Catholics, for they could always count upon service in the French army and possibly in the Spanish. The author then addresses himself to minor practical considerations, such as the question of whether French martial law will supersede Irish law within these newly formed groups of the French army while they remain resident in Ireland.

At only one point in this essay does the author allow himself to become ironical. Referring to this English permission given the French, he states: "Such a Method of providing for Persons, whose Principles render them unservicable in our Army, is indeed a little more charitable than a late Project for preventing Irish Children from being starv'd, by fattening them up and selling them to the Butcher." This obviously is an invitation to Swift to resume his pose as the Modest Proposer. He accepts the challenge and opens his "Answer" by taking literally the ironical sentence from the *Craftsman's* essay. Again Swift's Modest Proposer "humbly" puts forward a proposal for the betterment of Ireland at no expense to England: part of the annual crop of flesh (here, young Irishmen) should be exported by whatever prince will "bear the Carriage." England, having already closed all exports of Irish livestock, has graciously left open this one loop-hole for the exportation of an Irish product. The author of the essay in the *Craftsman* has come forward, unbidden, officiously to oppose this one remaining exportation of an Irish product. Swift sustains this ironic pose in this essay and continues the characterization of the Modest Proposer which he had created in "A Modest Proposal." Although "An Answer" does not so often strike fire and its irony is not so intensive and extensive as that of "A Modest Proposal," it can, in its less ambitious way and in its smaller scale, stand quite proudly with its more famous predecessor.

The course of Swiftian scholarship and criticism over the last two and one half centuries has indeed been uneven. Most of the eighteenth-century literary comments tend to deal with Swift's ideas and his character. Such a bold satirist is quite naturally often misunderstood as to his own character and motives, and several of his friends and one relative (Deane Swift) published what amount to apologias for the Dean and his works. Late in the century Dr. Johnson took a dim view of Swift's talent and character. None of these works is reprinted here because none deals with "A Modest Proposal," a fact which is in itself significant, perhaps indicating that other works by Swift (perhaps *A Tale of a Tub* and *Gulliver's Travels*) upset readers of his own century more than "A Modest Proposal" did.

With very few exceptions nineteenth-century critics, if they attended to Swift at all, were preoccupied with biographical matters

(Did Swift marry Stella? Was he insane?). The excerpt from Thackeray is reprinted here to reveal what a critically debilitating error it is grossly to confuse biography, personal bias, and literary criticism. (In this century some Freudians continue this school of criticism; however, no example is reprinted here because none deals directly and at any length with "A Modest Proposal.")

Sir Walter Scott and Sir Henry Craik are the two great exceptions to the general tone of the nineteenth-century criticism of Swift. Both men brought keen insight to some of Swift's works themselves; and both, especially Craik, have uncovered an unusual amount of simple historical data relevant to a comprehension of the works of Swift.

With the landmark publication of Ricardo Quintana's *The Mind and Art of Jonathan Swift* in 1936, Swiftian scholarship and criticism was finally set upon the path along which it still continues: away from the fruitless view of Swift as the mad genius savagely lashing out against mankind from his Irish exile and toward a serious analysis of the literary works themselves. The selections in this casebook offer a good range of the several kinds of scholarship and criticism now being applied to the study of the works of Swift: the historical, the biographical, the generic, the formal, and the kind of close analysis associated with the New Criticism.

A note on this edition of the text of the two essays by Swift printed here: they are modernized versions of the definitive text edited by Herbert Davis and appearing in *The Prose Works of Jonathan Swift*, Herbert Davis, General Editor, Volume XII (Oxford: Basil Blackwell, 1955). I have made the texts conform more to modern usage by reducing to lower case the capitalized common nouns and by using modern spelling. Except for proper nouns, I have retained Swift's extensive use of italics because of their variety of uses, the main ones being emphasis and tagging cant phrases. I wish to thank Sir Basil Blackwell, who holds the copyright of the texts cited above, for his permission to use the texts in the manner described.

A Modest Proposal
for Preventing the Children of Poor People in Ireland, from Being a Burden to Their Parents or Country; and for Making Them Beneficial to the Public

It is a melancholy object to those, who walk through this great town, or travel in the country; when they see the *streets*, the *roads*, and *cabin doors* crowded with *beggars* of the female sex, followed by three, four, or six children, *all in rags*, and importuning every passenger for an alms. These *mothers*, instead of being able to work for their honest livelihood, are forced to employ all their time in strolling to beg sustenance for their *helpless infants;* who, as they grow up, either turn *thieves* for want of work; or leave their *dear native country, to fight for the Pretender in Spain*, or sell themselves to the Barbadoes.

I think it is agreed by all parties, that this prodigious number of children in the arms, or on the backs, or at the *heels* of their *mothers*, and frequently of their *fathers*, is *in the present deplorable state of the kingdom*, a very great additional grievance; and therefore, whoever could find out a fair, cheap, and easy method of making these children sound and useful members of the commonwealth, would deserve so well of the public, as to have his statue set up for a preserver of the nation.

But my intention is very far from being confined to provide only for the children of *professed beggars:* it is of a much greater extent, and shall take in the whole number of infants at a certain age, who are born of parents, in effect as little able to support them, as those who demand our charity in the streets.

As to my own part, having turned my thoughts for many years, upon this important subject, and maturely weighed the several *schemes of other projectors*, I have always found them grossly mistaken in their computation. It is true a child, *just dropped from its dam*, may be supported by her milk, for a solar year with little other nourishment; at most not above the value of two shillings; which the mother may certainly get, or the value in *scraps*, by her lawful occupation of *begging:* and, it is exactly at one year old, that I propose to provide for them in such a manner, as, instead of being a charge upon

11

their *parents*, or the *parish*, or *wanting food and raiment* for the rest of their lives; they shall, on the contrary, contribute to the feeding, and partly to the clothing, of many thousands.

There is likewise another great advantage in my *scheme*, that it will prevent those *voluntary abortions*, and that horrid practice of *women murdering their bastard children*; alas! too frequent among us; sacrificing the *poor innocent babes*, I doubt, more to avoid the expense than the shame; which would move tears and pity in the most savage and inhuman breast.

The number of souls in Ireland being usually reckoned one million and a half; of these I calculate there may be about two hundred thousand couple whose wives are breeders; from which number I subtract thirty thousand couples, who are able to maintain their own children; although I apprehend there cannot be so many, under the *present distresses of the kingdom*; but this being granted, there will remain an hundred and seventy thousand breeders. I again subtract fifty thousand, for those women who miscarry, or whose children die by accident, or disease, within the year. There only remain an hundred and twenty thousand children of poor parents, annually born: the question therefore is, how this number shall be reared, and provided for? Which, as I have already said, under the present situation of affairs, is utterly impossible, by all the methods hitherto proposed: for we can *neither employ them in handicraft* or *agriculture*; we neither build houses, (I mean in the country) nor cultivate land: they can very seldom pick up a livelihood *by stealing* until they arrive at six years old; except where they are of towardly parts; although, I confess, they learn the rudiments much earlier; during which time, they can, however, be properly looked upon only as *probationers*; as I have been informed by a principal gentleman in the county of Cavan, who protested to me, that he never knew above one or two instances under the age of six, even in a part of the kingdom *so renowned for the quickest proficiency in that art*.

I am assured by our merchants, that a boy or a girl before twelve years old, is no saleable commodity; and even when they come to this age, they will not yield above three pounds, or three pounds and half a crown at most, on the exchange; which cannot turn to account either to the parents or the kingdom; the charge of nutriment and rags, having been at least four times that value.

I shall now therefore humbly propose my own thoughts; which I hope will not be liable to the least objection.

I have been assured by a very knowing American of my acquaintance in London; that a young healthy child, well nursed, is, at a year old, a most delicious, nourishing, and wholesome food; whether *stewed, roasted, baked,* or *boiled*; and, I make no doubt, that it will equally serve in a *fricasse,* or *ragout.*

I do therefore humbly offer it to *public consideration,* that of the hundred and twenty thousand children, already computed, whereof only one fourth part to be males; which is more than we allow to *sheep, black cattle,* or *swine*; and my reason is, that these children are seldom the fruits of marriage, a *circumstance not much regarded by our savages*; therefore, one male will be sufficient to serve *four females.* That the remaining hundred thousand, may, at a year old, be offered in sale to the *persons of quality* and *fortune,* through the kingdom; always advising the mother to let them suck plentifully in the last month, so as to render them plump, and fat for a good table. A child will make two dishes at an entertainment for friends; and when the family dines alone, the fore or hind quarter will make a reasonable dish; and seasoned with a little pepper or salt, will be very good boiled on the fourth day, especially in *winter.*

I have reckoned upon a medium, that a child just born will weigh twelve pounds; and in a solar year, if tolerably nursed, increases to twenty eight pounds.

I grant this food will be somewhat dear, and therefore very *proper for landlords*; who, as they have already devoured most of the parents, seem to have the best title to the children.

Infants flesh will be in season throughout the year; but more plentiful in March, and a little before and after: for we are told by a grave author, an eminent French physician, that *fish being a prolific diet,* there are more children born in *Roman Catholic countries* about nine months after Lent, than at any other season: therefore reckoning a year after Lent, the markets will be more glutted than usual; because the number of *Popish infants,* is, at least, three to one in this kingdom; and therefore it will have one other collateral advantage, by lessening the number of *Papists* among us.

I have already computed the charge of nursing a beggar's child (in which list I reckon all *cottagers, laborers,* and four fifths of the *farmers*) to be about two shillings *per annum,* rags included; and I believe, no gentleman would repine to give ten shillings for the *carcass of a good fat child*; which, as I have said, will make four dishes of excellent nutritive meat, when he has only some particular friend, or his own family, to dine with him. Thus the squire will learn to be a good landlord, and grow popular among his tenants; the mother will have eight shillings net profit, and be fit for work until she produces another child.

Those who are more thrifty *(as I must confess the times require)* may flay the carcass; the skin of which, artificially dressed, will make admirable *gloves for ladies,* and *summer boots for fine gentlemen.*

As to our city of Dublin; shambles may be appointed for this purpose, in the most convenient parts of it; and butchers we may be assured will not be wanting; although I rather recommend buying the children alive, and dressing them hot from the knife, as we do *roasting pigs.*

A very worthy person, *a true lover of his country,* and whose virtues I highly esteem, was lately pleased, in discoursing on this matter, to offer a refinement upon my scheme. He said, that many gentlemen of this kingdom, having of late destroyed their deer; he conceived, that the want of venison might be well supplied by the bodies of young lads and maidens, not exceeding fourteen years of age, nor under twelve; so great a number of both sexes in every county being now ready to starve, for want of work and service: and these to be disposed of by their parents, if alive, or otherwise by their nearest relations. But with due deference to so excellent a friend, and so deserving a patriot, I cannot be altogether in his sentiments. For as to the males, my American acquaintance assured me from frequent experience, that their flesh was generally tough and lean, like that of our school boys, by continual exercise, and their taste disagreeable; and to fatten them would not answer the charge. Then, as to the females, it would, I think, with humble submission, *be a loss to the public,* because they soon would become breeders themselves: and besides it is not improbable, that some scrupulous people might be apt to censure such a practice (although indeed very unjustly) as a little bordering upon cruelty; which, I confess, has always been with me the strongest objection against any project, how well soever intended.

But in order to justify my friend; he confessed, that this expedient was put into his head by the famous Salmanaazor, a native of the island of Formosa, who came from thence to London, above twenty years ago, and in conversation told my friend, that in his country, when any young person happened to be put to death, the executioner sold the carcass to *persons of quality,* as a prime dainty; and that, in his time, the body of a plump girl of fifteen, who was crucified for an attempt to poison the emperor, was sold to his *Imperial Majesty's prime Minister of State,* and other great Mandarins of the Court, *in joints from the gibbet,* at four hundred crowns. Neither indeed can I deny, that if the same use were made of several plump young girls in this town, who, without a single groat to their fortunes, cannot stir abroad without a chair, and appear at the *play-house*, and *assemblies* in foreign fineries, which they never will pay for; the kingdom would not be the worse.

Some persons of a desponding spirit are in great concern about that vast number of poor people, who are aged, diseased, or maimed; and I have been desired to employ my thoughts what course may be taken, to ease the nation of so grievous an incumbrance. But I am not in the least pain upon that matter; because it is very well known, that they are every day *dying*, and *rotting*, by *cold* and *famine*, and *filth*, and *vermin*, as fast as can be reasonably expected. And as to the younger laborers, they are now in almost as hopeful a condition: they cannot get work, and consequently pine away for want of nourishment, to a degree that if at any time they are accidentally hired to common labor, they have not strength to perform it; and thus the country, and themselves, are in a fair way of being soon delivered from the evil to come.

I have too long digressed; and therefore shall return to my subject. I think the advantages by the proposal which I have made, are obvious, and many, as well as of the highest importance.

For, *first*, as I have already observed, it would greatly lessen the *number of Papists*, with whom we are yearly over-run; being the principal breeders of the nation, as well as our most dangerous enemies; and who stay home on purpose, with a design to *deliver the kingdom to the Pretender*; hoping to take their advantage by the absence of *so many good Protestants*, who have chosen rather to leave their country, than stay at home, and pay tithes against their conscience, to an idolatrous *Episcopal Curate*.

Secondly, the poorer tenants will have something valuable of their own, which, by law, may be made liable to distress, and help pay their landlord's rent; their corn and cattle being already seized, and *money a thing unknown*.

Thirdly, whereas the maintenance of an hundred thousand children, from two years old, and upwards, cannot be computed at less than ten shillings a piece *per annum*, the nation's stock will be thereby increased fifty thousand pounds *per annum*; besides the profit of a new dish, introduced to the tables of all *gentlemen of fortune* in the kingdom, who have any refinement in taste; and the money will circulate among ourselves, the goods being entirely of our own growth and manufacture.

Fourthly, the constant breeders, besides the gain of eight shillings *sterling per annum*, by the sale of their children, will be rid of the charge of maintaining them after the first year.

Fifthly, this food would likewise bring great *custom to taverns,* where the vintners will certainly be so prudent, as to procure the best recipes for dressing it to perfection; and consequently, have their houses frequented by all the *fine gentlemen,* who justly value themselves upon their knowledge in good eating; and a skillful cook, who understands how to oblige his guests, will contrive to make it as expensive as they please.

Sixthly, this would be a great inducement to marriage, which all wise nations have either encouraged by rewards, or enforced by laws and penalties. It would encrease the care and tenderness of mothers toward their children, when they were sure of a settlement for life, to the poor babes, provided in some sort by the public, to their annual profit, instead of expense. We should soon see an honest emulation among the married women, *which of them could bring the fattest child to the market.* Men would become as *fond* of their wives. during the time of their pregnancy, as they are now of their *mares* in foal, their *cows* in calf, or *sows* when they are ready to farrow; nor offer to beat or kick them, (as it is too *frequent* a practice) for fear of a miscarriage.

Many other advantages might be enumerated. For instance, the addition of some thousand carcasses in our exportation of barrelled beef: the propagation of *swines flesh,* and improvement in the art of making good *bacon;* so much wanted among us by the great destruction of *pigs,* too frequent at our tables, and are no way comparable in taste, or magnificence, to a well-grown fat yearling child; which roasted whole, will make a considerable figure at a *Lord Mayor's feast,* or any other public entertainment. But this, and many others, I omit; being studious of brevity.

Supposing that one thousand families in this city, would be constant customers for infants flesh; besides others who might have it at *merry meetings,* particularly *weddings* and *Christenings;* I compute that Dublin would take off, annually, about twenty thousand carcasses; and the rest of the kingdom (where probably they will be sold somewhat cheaper) the remaining eighty thousand.

I can think of no one objection, that will possibly be raised against this proposal; unless it should be urged, that the number of people will be thereby much lessened in the kingdom. This I freely own; and it was indeed one principal design in offering it to the world. I desire the reader will observe, that I calculate my remedy *for this one individual kingdom of Ireland, and for no other that ever was, is, or I think ever can be upon earth.* Therefore, let no man talk to me of other expedients: *of taxing our absentees at five shillings a pound: of using neither clothes, nor household furniture except what is of our own growth and manufacture: of utterly rejecting the materials and instruments that promote foreign luxury: of curing the expensiveness of pride, idleness, and gaming in our women: of introducing a vein of parsimony, prudence, and temperance: of learning to love our country, wherein we differ even from Laplanders, and the inhabitants of Topinamboo: of quitting our animosities, and factions; nor act any longer like the Jews, who were murdering one another at the very moment their city was taken: of being a little cautious not to sell our country and consciences for nothing: of teaching landlords to have, at least, one degree of mercy towards their tenants. Lastly, of putting a spirit of honesty, industry, and skill into our shop-keepers; who, if a resolution could now be taken to buy only our native goods, would immediately unite to cheat and exact upon us in the price, the measure, and the goodness; nor could ever yet be brought to make one fair proposal of just dealing, though often and earnestly invited to it.*

Therefore I repeat, let no man talk to me of these and the like expedients; till he has, at least, a glimpse of hope, that there will ever be some hearty and sincere attempt to put *them in practice.*

But, as to myself; having been wearied out for many years with offering vain, idle, visionary thoughts; and at length utterly despairing of success, I fortunately fell upon this proposal; which, as it is wholly new, so it has something *solid* and *real,* of no expense, and little trouble, full in our own power; and whereby we can incur no danger in *disobliging England:* for, this kind of commodity will not bear exportation; the flesh being of too tender a consistence, to admit a long continuance in salt; *although, perhaps, I could name a country, which would be glad to eat up our whole nation without it.*

After all, I am not so violently bent upon my own opinion, as to reject any offer proposed by wise men, which shall be found equally innocent, cheap, easy, and effectual. But before something of that kind shall be advanced, in contradiction to my scheme, and offering a better; I desire the author, or authors, will be pleased maturely to consider two points. *First,* as things now stand, how they will be able to find food and raiment, for a hundred thousand useless mouths and backs? and *secondly,* there being a round million of creatures in human figure, throughout this kingdom; whose whole subsistence, put into a common stock, would leave them in debt two millions of pounds *sterling;* adding those, who are beggars by profession, to the bulk of farmers, cottagers, and laborers, with their wives and children, who are beggars in effect; I desire those politicians, who dislike my overture, and may perhaps be so bold as to attempt an answer, that they will first ask the parents of these mortals, whether they would not, at this day, think it a great happiness to have been sold for food at a year old, in the manner I prescribe; and thereby have avoided such a perpetual scene of misfortunes, as they have since gone through; by the *oppression of landlords*; the impossibility of paying rent, without money or trade; the want of common sustenance, with neither house nor clothes, to cover them from the inclemencies of weather; and the most inevitable prospect of entailing the like, of greater miseries upon their breed for ever.

I profess, in the sincerity of my heart, that I have not the least personal interest, in endeavoring to promote this necessary work; having no other motive than the *public good of my country, by advancing our trade, providing for infants, relieving the poor, and giving some pleasure to the rich.* I have no children, by which I can propose to get a single penny; the youngest being nine years old, and my wife past child-bearing.

William Makepeace Thackeray

From The English Humourists of the Eighteenth Century*

It is my belief that he [Swift] suffered frightfully from the consciousness of his own scepticism, and that he had bent his pride so far down as to put his apostasy out to hire.[1] The paper left behind him, called "Thoughts on Religion," is merely a set of excuses for not professing disbelief. He says of his sermons that he preached pamphlets: they have scarce a Christian characteristic; they might be preached from the steps of a synagogue, or the floor of a mosque, or the box of a coffee-house almost. There is little or no cant — he is too great and too proud for that; and, in so far as the badness of his sermons goes, he is honest. But having put that cassock on, it poisoned him: he was strangled in his bands. He goes through life, tearing, like a man possessed with a devil. Like Abudah in the Arabian story, he is always looking out for the Fury, and knows that the night will come and the inevitable hag with it. What a night, my God, it was! what a lonely rage and long agony — what a vulture that tore the heart of that giant![2] It is awful to think of the great sufferings of this great man. Through life he always seems alone, somehow. Goethe was so. I cannot fancy Shakespeare other-/31/wise. The giants must live apart. The kings can have no company. But this man suffered so; and deserved

*Reprinted from William Makepeace Thackeray, *The English Humourists of the Eighteenth Century* (London: Smith, Elder & Company, 1869), pp. 30–33.

[1] "Mr. Swift lived with him [Sir William Temple] some time, but resolving to settle himself in some way of living, was inclined to take orders. However, although his fortune was very small, he had a scruple of entering into the Church merely for support."—*Anecdotes of the Family of Swift*, by the DEAN.

[2] "Dr. Swift had a natural severity of face, which even his smiles could never soften, or his utmost gaiety render placid and serene; but when that sternness of visage was increased by rage, it is scarce possible to imagine looks or features that carried in them more terror and austerity."—ORRERY.

so to suffer. One hardly reads anywhere of such a pain.

The "saeva indignatio" of which he spoke as lacerating his heart, and which he dares to inscribe on his tombstone — as if the wretch who lay under that stone waiting God's judgment had a right to be angry — breaks out from him in a thousand pages of his writings, and tears and rends him. Against men in office, he having been over-thrown; against men in England, he having lost his chance of pre-ferment there, the furious exile never fails to rage and curse. Is it fair to call the famous "Drapier's Letters" patriotism? They are master-pieces of dreadful humour and invective: they are reasoned logically enough too, but the proposition is as monstrous and fabulous as the Lilliputian island. It is not that the grievance is so great, but there is his enemy — the assault is wonderful for its activity and terrible rage. It is Samson, with a bone in his hand, rushing on his enemies and felling them: one admires not the cause so much as the strength, the anger, the fury of the champion. As is the case with madmen, certain subjects provoke him, and awaken his fits of wrath. Marriage is one of these; in a hundred passages in his writings he rages against it; rages against children — an object of constant satire, even more con-temptible in his eyes than a lord's chaplain, is a poor curate with a large family. The idea of this luckless paternity never fails to bring down from him gibes and foul language. Could Dick Steele, or Gold-smith, or Fielding, in his most reckless moment of satire, have written anything like the Dean's famous "modest proposal" for eating chil-dren? Not one of these but/32/melts at the thoughts of childhood, fon-dles and caresses it. Mr. Dean has no such softness, and enters the nursery with the tread and gaiety of an ogre.[3] "I have been assured," says he in the "Modest Proposal," "by a very knowing American of my acquaintance in London, that a young healthy child, well-nursed, is, at a year old, a most delicious, nourishing, and wholesome food, whether stewed, roasted, baked, or boiled; and I make no doubt it will equally serve in a *ragout*." And, taking up this pretty joke, as his way is, he argues it with perfect gravity and logic.

He turns and twists this subject in a score of different ways: he hashes it; and he serves it up cold; and he garnishes it; and relishes it always. He describes the little animal as "dropped from its dam," advising that the mother should let it suck plentifully in the last

---

[3] "*London, April 10th*, 1713. "Lady Masham's eldest boy is very ill: I doubt he will not live, and she stays at Kensington to nurse him, which vexes us all. She is so excessively fond, it makes me mad. She should never leave the Queen, but leave everything, to stick to what is so much the interest of the public, as well as her own" . . . . —*Journal.*

month, so as to render it plump and fat for a good table! "A child," says his reverence, "will make two dishes at an entertainment for friends; and when the family dines alone, the fore or hindquarter will make a reasonable dish," and so on; and, the subject being so delightful that he cannot leave it — he proceeds to recommend, in place of venison for squires' tables, "the bodies of young lads and maidens not exceeding fourteen nor under twelve." Amiable humourist! laughing castigator of morals! There was a process well known and practised in the Dean's gay days: when a lout entered the coffee-house, the wags proceeded to what they called "roast-/33/ing" him. This is roasting a subject with a vengeance. The Dean had a native genius for it. As the "Almanach des Gourmands" says, *On naît rôtisseur.*

And it was not merely by the sarcastic method that Swift exposed the unreasonableness of loving and having children. In Gulliver, the folly of love and marriage by graver arguments and advice. In the famous Lilliputian kingdom, Swift speaks with approval of the practice of instantly removing children from their parents and educating them by the State; and amongst his favourite horses, a pair of foals are stated to be the very utmost a well-regulated equine couple would permit themselves. In fact, our great satirist was of opinion that conjugal love was unadvisable, and illustrated the theory by his own practice and example — God help him — which made him about the most wretched being in God's world.[4]

---

[4] "My health is somewhat mended, but at best I have an ill head and an aching heart."—In May, 1719.

Sir Henry Craik

From The Life of Jonathan Swift, Dean of St. Patrick's Dublin*

Nothing shows Swift's genius in these Irish tracts more conclusively than the marvellously simple materials with which he maintains their force. He enters into the questions with no intricacy, he treats them with no variety of view. Setting aside all those tracts which careful scrutiny shows to be falsely ascribed to Swift, it is surprising how small is the range amongst the rest.[1] They have all one end and one aim: "Be independent." Law cannot help: theory is futile: English selfishness has left us little. But if we can gain anything we can gain it by self-assertion, and by that alone. Swift is quite well acquainted with the current nostrums. He names almost all of them. He speaks of Prior with approbation.[2] He deals out a patronizing nod to this or that scheme. But he never lingers long over any one. He saw that the evil lay deeper, and that it could be cured only by giving to Ireland the motive power of independence, by kindling her energy through withering sarcasm, derisive scorn, and fiercest indignation. The sarcasm and the indignation are for the English selfishness: the scorn for Irish imbecility and weakness. He repeats over and over again the

---

*Reprinted from Sir Henry Craik, *The Life of Jonathan Swift, Dean of St. Patrick's Dublin* (London: John Murray, 1882), pp. 413–416.

[1]This is a matter which could be fully dealt with only in re-editing the works. But again it must be pointed out, that we should err widely in accepting all the tracts as genuine which Scott's edition attributes to Swift. The descriptive notes, which preface the tracts in that edition, are frequently contradicted by the tracts themselves. On the authority of that odd pedant, Dr. Barrett, tracts are accepted by Scott's amanuensis, which are often inconsistent with Swift's views, feeble travesties of his style, and which scarcely pretend even to imitate his wit.

[2]*Proposal that the Ladies wear Irish Manufactures.* See Scott's Swift, (2nd edit.) vol. VII. p. 260.

same advice. "Quit yourselves like men, be strong. Curb your follies, and resist the fantastic taste for foreign luxuries. Know that your strength is in the plough and not in the depopulated pasture lands." "Ajax was mad, when he mistook a flock of sheep for his enemies: but we shall never be sober until we have the same way of thinking."

Perhaps the greatest, certainly the most characteristic, of Swift's efforts in this direction, is his *"Modest Proposal for pre-/414/venting the Children of Poor People in Ireland from being a burden to their Parents or the Country."* It was published in 1729, when, even from Archbishop Boulter's letters, we learn that people were starving in hundreds through the famine, and that the dead were left unburied before their own doors. English civilization was shamed by the sight, and to Swift at least it seemed no moment to be silent. His sarcasm was never applied with more deadly seriousness of purpose. With the grave and decent self-respect of a reformer, who knows the value of the proposal he has to make, Swift propounds his scheme. There is no strain in the language with which the state of matters is described: but the very simplicity and matter-of-fact tone that are assumed, make the description all the more telling. Of a million and a half inhabitants, about two hundred thousand may be the number of those who are bringing children into the world: of these about thirty thousand can provide for their children. There remain one hundred and seventy thousand whose case has to be met: and the pamphlet assumes as an admitted truth, that no method yet proposed can meet that case. Agriculture and handicrafts, we have not: and though stealing offers an employment, yet complete proficiency in that calling is not often attained under the age of six. What then has to be done?

With the calm deliberation of a statistician calculating the food supply of the country, Swift brings forward his suggestion. He has inquired into the facts: and finds that a well-grown child of a year old, is a most delicious, nourishing, and wholesome food, whether stewed, roasted, baked, or boiled: and he makes no doubt that it will equally serve in a fricassee or a ragout. The charge for nourishing such a child, in the present scale, will be about two shillings per annum, "rags included:" and "he believes no gentleman will repine to give ten shillings for the carcase of a good fat child." The mother will have eight shillings net profit.

In the same tone, he dilates upon the advantages of the/415/ scheme. Refinements have been suggested to him. The flesh of young lads and maidens, too, might, it is thought, be put to the same use. But with all respect, he sees difficulties: and chiefly because "some scrupulous persons might be apt to censure such a practice (though

indeed very unjustly) as a little bordering upon cruelty: which, I
confess, has always been with me the strongest objection against any
project, how well soever intended." As he concludes with an earnest,
but modest enforcement of his scheme, he is careful to add that he
has no personal motive; his own children are all past the age when
he could make a profit of them.

No work of Swift's has been more canvassed: none more variously
estimated: and none more grievously misunderstood. Some have
esteemed it a heartless piece of ridicule, a callous laugh raised out
of abject misery. Men who might have been expected to see more
clearly, have shuddered in well-simulated horror, at a cynicism which
they have found too strong for their nerves. So to interpret it, is to
misread it as entirely as the Frenchman did, who took it as a grave
and practical suggestion, and who fancied that Swift in sober earnest
proposed that infants in Ireland should be used for food. In truth,
the ridicule is but a thin disguise. From beginning to end, it is laden
with grave and torturing bitterness. Each touch of calm and ghastly
humour, is added with the gravity of the surgeon who probes a wound
to the quick. Swift's clearness of vision laid the woes of Ireland bare
to him; he has left them on record for all time. Molesworth, and
Dobbs, and Prior, and Browne, are all forgotten: can England ever
forget what lies on her conscience, while Swift's *Modest Proposal*
continues to be read?

Alongside of the *Modest Proposal* we may read another tract which
has much the same character, though with application more restricted.
In 1730, the *Craftsman* had made some strong remarks on the facil-
ities recently given for the recruiting of the French army in Ireland.
The incident, as we/416/ see from Archbishop Boulter's letters,[3] had
caused some alarm amongst the Government adherents, who found
their own transaction wearing an untoward aspect. The *Craftsman*
had seized the opportunity: and Swift, whose sympathies were with
the *Craftsman*, added to the agitation by his ironical reply. "Why
hinder the recruiting?" he asks, in all simplicity. "Do you not know
how the loss of these recruits will benefit Ireland? Elsewhere, no doubt,
men are the sinews of a nation: but this is a maxim 'controlled' in
Ireland. What we want is depopulation. Make Ireland a desert, and
all will be well. Have a grazier and his family for every 2000 acres,
and then we shall be as England wishes us to be. If the army is idle,
let it find employment in gathering taxes. If we still need more deple-
tion, take our surplus to the colonies and employ them as a screen

---

[3]See Boulter's *Letters*, vol II, p. 30.

between his Majesty's subjects and their savage neighbours. When our island is a desert, we will send all our raw material to England, and receive from her all our manufactured articles. A leather coinage will be all we want, separated, as we shall then be, from all human kind. We shall have lost all: but we may be left in peace, as we shall have no more to tempt the plunderer." The *Modest Proposal* has had thousands of readers for one that this *Answer to the Craftsman* has had. The former needs no such knowledge of Irish affairs for its apprehension: but, special as is its object, the irony of the *Answer* is as perfect in its way.

Ricardo Quintana

Situational Satire:
A Commentary on the Method
of Swift*

Much depends on the readiness with which we acknowledge the
element of impersonality in literary art. The impersonality of drama
we perceive and accept instinctively, since our normal responses to a
play are grounded in this very acceptance. We do not confuse the
dramatist with his characters; unless we are Romantic critics writing
on Shakespeare, we do not take the play as direct expression of the
writer's personality. The play stands forth as an artifice; we are willing
to think of it and discuss it in terms of structural form. How different
in this respect our reactions are to most non-dramatic forms of literary
art can be measured by the degree to which we confound the writer
and the written work. When we see the work and its author as inter-
changeable, when we take the work to be an act at the level of every-
day behaviour, we have pretty well lost sight of the impersonal element
and the presence of anything in the nature of deliberate method and
form. For such reasons we often find it hard to come to terms with
the lyric poem as a poem, as a construct, with the result that much
of our commentary on poetry turns out to be either description of
our impressions or reconstruction—largely imaginary—of a precise
moment in the poet's emotional history with which we have chosen
to equate the poem. Perhaps we find it hardest of all to admit of any
distinction between a satirist and his satiric composition—and this
despite the fact that satire is much more obviously a form of rhetoric
than is lyric poetry. It is scarcely surprising, therefore, that Swift's

*Reprinted from the *University of Toronto Quarterly*, XVII, (January, 1948),
130-136, by permission of the author and the publisher. Copyright 1948 by the University of Toronto Press.

satiric method, which everywhere stares us in the face, is only dimly recognized to be a method. We praise Swift's style; we speak of his use of allegory and his mastery of disgust; but we do not follow through with conviction. Sooner or later we allow the personality of Swift to take over and in consequence to obscure the artist, the craftsman, who after all is only Jonathan Swift's distant relative.

It is perfectly apparent—and here is a key that will unlock the first door—that in every one of Swift's more notable prose satires we have a fictional character or group of characters: Lemuel Gulliver; Isaac Bickerstaff; M. B., Drapier; the humanitarian projector who writes *A Modest Proposal*; the three brothers in the *Tale of a Tub*. What we refuse to see is that Swift himself is *not* present, that it is the characters who are in complete charge. Swift's method is uniformly by way of dramatic satire. He creates a fully realized character and a fully realized world for him to move in. Sometimes, as in *Gulliver's Travels,* the satiric action is developed in terms of the character's reactions to this world; but frequently the action/131/is of essentially another sort, deriving from the crazy assurance with which the character makes himself at home in his cloud-cuckoo-land, tidies the place up, and proceeds to enlarge the bounds of his estate. The difference referred to is a real one, a genuine difference of method, something much more ponderable than the words which must be used to describe it. It is the difference between Gulliver and Bickerstaff, between the *Travels* and the Partridge-Bickerstaff Papers. Gulliver is a reluctant explorer, cast by storms and tides upon strange countries where he is compelled to live at the mercy of the inhabitants. Isaac Bickerstaff, by contrast, is at the mercy of nothing: he assumes such complete control over the laws of logic and astrology that he does not hesitate to condemn a man to death and carry out the sentence.

The latter method is more characteristic of Swift than the method employed in *Gulliver's Travels*. Both are dramatic in the sense suggested, consisting of the depiction of characters and worlds, the character being sometimes projected into a world prepared for him in advance, but more often being allowed to create one for himself. It is in regard to the character's creation of his own world that we begin to suspect that something more than what we ordinarily think of as a dramatic method has perhaps entered into the compositions of Swift. In the *Tale of a Tub* we hear of "many famous discoveries, projects, and machines," of noteworthy devices, of arts highly useful to the commonwealth. In point of fact, the entire *Tale* and its accompanying *Discourse concerning the Mechanical Operation of the Spirit* are one long series of projects, devices, and machines, spun out with amazing

bravura. What was there about projectors and projects that so fascinated this particular satiric artist?

II

Before pressing on in further search of Swift's satiric method, we
ought perhaps to establish our larger view. The misinterpretation of
Swift is proverbial, but with fewer exceptions than is sometimes realized those who have written about him have fought energetically
against the deep-lying prejudices of the sort voiced so deplorably and
so brilliantly by Thackeray. It happens that we know a good deal of
both the private life of Swift and his public career, and much about
his motives, interests, prejudices, and theoretical convictions. Criticism, as distinct from biography, is concerned to find the relationship
between the man and the artist, but this it can do with some degree
of effectiveness only through a sense of the general problem. How do
the writer as man and the writer as artist stand to one another? Where
does personality end and impersonality begin?

Satire, as much as and no less than drama and lyric poetry, is a
construct. It is precisely devised literary composition, a form of rhetoric. It may proceed, as we have seen, by way of characters whose
actions are recorded objectively or who speak as in a play; but even
in the absence of such/132/ikons there is still the assumed character
of the satirist, which despite a convincingly deceptive egotism is quite
as much an imaginative creation as any ikon. Nor, in another and
more vital respect, is there any substantial difference between satire
on the one hand and drama and lyric poetry on the other. Each of
these fashions its own world, not as Swift creates the land of the
Houyhnhnms or Shakespeare the island of Prospero, but rather in the
sense that *Gulliver's Travels*—all of it—is a world, that *The Tempest*
—the play as a totality—is its own, complete universe. This special
world is a most complex structure, having a logic of its own which
governs feeling and speech. It is at once a way of looking at things,
a way of feeling, and a way of speaking.

The writer himself, the man with a human character and practical
motives, is present of course, but he stands several levels away from
this manner of feeling and speech. The avowed intention of the satirist
is to expose folly and evil and to castigate them, and there is no satire
worthy of the name which does not in fact establish a moral dichot-
omy: right over against wrong, rectified vision or virtue against twisted
vision, human dignity and freedom against stupidity, blindness, per-
versity. If the moral sense of some satirists—of Byron, for instance—

seems elementary, the moral sense of Swift we recognize as that in-
herited from the humanist tradition, in which man's freedom was
defined in terms of ethical responsibility and in accord with the
Christian awareness of human incapacity and failure. The drift of
Swift's satiric statements, their intellectual-ethical significance, the
practical effects they were designed to achieve are made clear by the
history of the age and our knowledge of Swift's character. The impact
of his satires is another problem, for their meaning as satiric con-
structs embraces something which is more than their practical meaning and qualitatively different from it. What this other thing is, is the
question, or rather, how to find the terms which will enable us to
talk about it without evasion. It is a way of thought and feeling, but
only as it is a method—a tone, a style, a manner of execution—can
it be described in the language which criticism must come to when
it seeks to put close observation in the place of impressionism.

III

It is essential to sense the fact that the method of Swift is a good
deal more than what we often think of as a method. Fundamentally,
it is an imaginative point of view, making possible and controlling a
kind of translation into terms peculiar to a certain angle of perception. This means that it cannot be exclusively identified with any
single procedure or device however characteristic of Swift. Though
dramatic construction marks all of his best-known satiric works, it
would be a mistake to regard such construction as the gist of the
matter. Similarly, we have to resist any temptation to single out Swift's
use of allegory or of parody in an effort to isolate his method. All of
these devices operate together; they are modes/133/of expression
within a single language; they are functions of something larger. What
name we find for this enclosing method is not particularly important,
since there is no precise term that can do all the necessary work.
Situational satire will serve.

A satire of Swift's is, we may say, an exhibited situation or series
of such situations. Once the situation has been suggested, once its tone,
its flavour have been given, it promptly takes command of itself and
proceeds to grow and organize by virtue of its own inherent principles.
It is a state of affairs within which, as we mistakenly put it, "anything
can happen"—mistakenly because everything that does happen is
instantly recognized as a part of *this*, a unique situation. Nevertheless,
the room for self-improvisation seems limitless, and the comic scale
ranges from the hilarious to the grim. It is to be observed that the
satirist is himself not involved: he is as much an observer, as much

outside all the fuss and nonsense, as we are. (Is it this that we mean when, in speaking of the satires, we comment on the "coldness of Swift"? We know that he was not cold, else we should not be quoting his epitaph as we do.) For the incidents which come to pass no one can be held responsible, any more than for the ideas and emotions which appear. What we have is, literally, an exhibition: everything is shown; everything is at least one degree removed from reality. In short, the situation may be thought of as a kind of chamber within which ideas and emotions are made to move and collide at accelerated speed.

With a recognition of the situation as such comes a perception of the functional character of Swift's favourite devices, which serve both in the creation of the situation and in the generation of the kinetic energy by which it is sustained. There are at least five of these devices that strike us forcibly: drama by way of created characters; parody, or at any rate the imitation of a specific literary *genre*; allegory; the "myth"; and "discoveries, projects, and machines." Of the first of these enough has already been said. Nor is it necessary to dwell at length on Swift's use of parody; we find epic parody in the closing passages of the *Battle*, parody of modern scribblers throughout the *Tale*, parody of the projector's pamphlet in the *Modest Proposal*, and the faithful reproduction, in *Gulliver's Travels*, of the style, tone, and matter-of-fact reporting found in the genuine travel-books of the time. Parody is in itself so close to the dramatic method that the two are sometimes difficult to distinguish; in Swift, parody is only another means of creating and exploiting a situation having its own unmistakable thickness. The world which the *Modest Proposal* invites us to live in is our own familiar world twice refracted, our world as remade in the enthusiastic imagination of a typical projector, and that remade world further distorted through parody.

Allegory in Swift's satires is really of two sorts. When it sets up a recognizable parallelism between two systems of events or ideas it derives quite directly from the kind of allegory which was constantly being used by post-Restoration writers in commenting on contemporary events. The/134/political allegory running through *Gulliver's Travels* is of this nature. Much the same are the short fable (the spider-bee episode in the *Battle*) and the extended fable (the story of the animated books in the *Battle* and the story of the three brothers in the *Tale*). The whole point of allegory thus employed lies in clear correspondence, one set of details suggesting and interpreting another set. But if we agree that the *Mechanical Operation of the Spirit* is "by way of allegory," we find ourselves confronted by something that does not fully answer to this kind of running parallelism. In this latter satiric fragment, attached to the *Tale* and the *Battle*, we are reminded that Mahomet refused fiery chariots, winged horses, and celestial sedans, and "would be borne to Heaven upon nothing but his ass"; and to go on "by way of allegory," we are asked to use, for the term *ass*, that of *gifted* or *enlightened teacher* and for *rider, fanatic auditory*. In this case, it seems, almost any parallelism no matter how fantastic will serve, since what is required is only an initial correspondence. The "allegory" does not throw light; rather, it is a challenge in response to which there arises a crazy world where religious fervour is created by mechanical means. And even where Swift is using allegory for sustained correspondence, one sometimes observes that the emerging situation tends to assert its independence. In the *Tale of a Tub,* for instance, the allegorical base on which the story of the three brothers rests never drops from sight, but with Peter and again with Jack we have an exuberant and perverted sense of power, of capacity to improvise and invent, which though in accord with the religious allegory is altogether in excess of it.

What have been called Swift's "myths" are familiar to every reader of the satires. Thus, it is the animal myth which informs both the *Modest Proposal* and the fourth book of *Gulliver's Travels*. Others appear in the *Tale of a Tub,* giving us that sect who worship tailors because of a belief that the universe is a large suit of clothes, the Aeolists who affirm "the gift of belching to be the noblest act of a rational creature," and the philosophical system which holds that all notable achievements are the result of madness. The Hobbian myth is of frequent occurrence: a set of principles, a practical programme, worked out from the assumption that man is a physical mechanism, his acts a phase not of intelligence but solely of matter. It is this kind of systematized make-believe, a nonsensical "as is," that gives life to the latter part of Gulliver's description of the Grand Academy of Lagado (Book III, chapter VI), where we are told of that school of political projectors whose admirable practices result from a clear understanding of the strict universal resemblance between the natural and the political body.

In what sense are these expanded metaphors to be taken as myths? The distinctive character of Swift's intuition, of his imaginative grasp of the human dilemma, is a moral realism which renounces with superb pride any mythological vision of human destiny. Only the fool believes he can see better through coloured glasses. The burden of civilization can be/135/borne solely by such as have learned that human dignity is achieved not through hope but through wilful disillusion, acceptance, resolution. If one sought to be paradoxical, one could say that the only myth genuinely embraced by Swift is the myth that there are no myths, the myth for which he found many statements, all of them variants of the single theme of the outside vs. the inside. "Last week I saw a woman flayed, and you will hardly believe how much it altered her person for the worse." This moral realism, emphasizing so mordantly and so insistently the deceptive fairness of the surface in contrast with what lies inside, was with Swift a passionate belief. Its metaphorical expressions, however, are less in the nature of myths than anti-myths, being in fact a kind of parody with a grim and earnest purpose. As statements they are designed to narrow, to shrink, not to enlarge.

The myths previously referred to (the Hobbian myth, etc.) are clearly of the fantastic order, and often blend into those "discoveries, projects, and machines" of which so much is said in the satires. Indeed, what for the projector himself is a cherished myth is for us an anti-myth, a machine, art, or device concocted in that madhouse which is the enthusiast's brain. The myth and the project, no less than dramatic form, parody, and allegory, are means whereby situations are brought about.

IV

That the method we have been speaking of appears for the first time in the great satire published in 1704, comprising the *Tale*, the *Battle*, and the *Mechanical Operation*, and not at all in the earlier Pindaric odes, written during the first years at Moor Park, is perhaps a sufficient reminder that Swift attained artistic maturity when he discovered and put on a hitherto unknown personality, a non-self who spoke and therefore thought a new idiom. The assurance which marks every passage of the 1704 satire is of one who has found creative freedom by learning how to avoid direct participation. The comedy of ideas, the self-developing irony of the situation require no intervention. Yet somehow, in this comedy that enacts itself and improvises its own language, Swift's passionate intuition has found its proper form.

Though each of the satires included in the 1704 volume is in itself an unmistakable comedy, we must not miss the larger comedy presented by the book as a whole, which by bringing the *Tale*, the *Battle of the Books*, and the *Mechanical Operation* into forced relationship establishes a context within which the three pieces are to be construed. Everything about them, the forms they are cast in, the deplorable gaps in the text, the marginal notes, the impertinence with which they ask to be taken as a trilogy, is part of this inclusive situation.

From this time on the method so brilliantly sustained in *A Tale of a Tub* becomes a part of Swift. It is his *alter ego*, his personality as prose satirist. Seen from the outside (how else can analysis view it?) it is method at the/136/lower level of stratagem, and Swift knew he had fashioned something in the way of comic technique. "There is one thing," he wrote in the "Apology" (1710) for the *Tale*, "which the judicious reader cannot but have observed, that some of those passages in this discourse . . . are what they call parodies, where the author personates the style and manner of other writers, whom he has a mind to expose." That it is far more than technique, that it is imagination and intuition, we acknowledge consciously or otherwise through our response to the satiric work of Swift taken as a whole— consciously when we recognize the presence of the artist, instinctively when we think we see a soul writhing in indignation.

Because the method of Swift is more than anything else a creative perception it cannot be summarized. Its essence is its history, its occurrence under different modes in the satires which came to be written. It operates in one fashion in *Gulliver's Travels,* notably in Books I, II, and IV (the comparative ineffectiveness of the third book being attributable to a relaxation of the method save in those passages concerning the virtuosi and the Struldbrugs). We can find it in the Drapier Letters: "They say 'Squire C—y has *Sixteen Thousand Pounds a Year,* now if he sends for the *Rent* to Town, as it is likely he does, he must have *Two Hundred and Forty Horses* to bring up his *Half Years Rent. . . .*" There is nothing to stop such ready calculation, and we shortly find ourselves with £40,000 and 1,200 horses on our hands. Leslie Stephen, speaking with the gravity of a cabinet minister, took exception to the economic heresies which gave rise to such arithmetic. But the Drapier was right, after all. Walpole and Wood were forcing on Ireland a monetary situation that was preposterous. The Drapier's inspired vision of a team of 1,200 horses drawing £40,000—all in copper halfpennies—about the streets of Dublin was no mere Irish myth.

Two final instances of the method. *An Argument against Abolishing Christianity* can perhaps be adequately described as ironic disputation. However, it is disputation that is more than a colloquy between A (who views abolition with concern) and B (all who, for various reasons, would abolish). A is likewise a multiplicity of voices, each point of view that is pressed into service carrying with it a somewhat different personality. It is a dialogue between the speaker's various selves, each of whom has a myth wherewith to confound his adversary;

the full pattern of the "argument" emerges solely from eccentric points of reference.

If the *Argument* is Erasmian (and Platonic), *A Modest Proposal* is pure Swift. Nowhere else is the method clearer, nowhere else is the fusion of moral insight and imaginative translation so complete. It is a character in action, a parody, a project, and an animal myth all at once, a situation within which any distinction between art and propaganda seems meaningless.

Louis A. Landa

A Modest Proposal and
Populousness*

Shortly before or after the publication of *A Modest Proposal* (1729)
—the exact date is uncertain—Swift wrote a tract entitled *Maxims
controlled in Ireland,* in which he examined "certain maxims of state,
founded upon long observation and experience, drawn from the constant practice of the wisest nations, and from the very principles of
government."[1] His purpose was to demonstrate that however much
these maxims applied to other countries they had no application to
Ireland. Among the maxims examined and confuted is one that was
cherished by the mercantilist economic writers of the last half of the
seventeenth and the first half of the eighteenth centuries: that people
are the riches of a nation. The passage in which this maxim is presented would seem to be the germ of *A modest proposal:*

> It is another undisputed maxim in government, 'That people
> are the riches of a nation'; which is so universally granted, that it
> will be hardly pardonable to bring it in doubt. And I will grant
> it to be so far true, even in this island, that if we had the African
> custom, or privilege, of selling our useless bodies for slaves to
> foreigners, it would be the most useful branch of our trade, by
> ridding us of a most unsupportable burthen, and bringing us
> money in the stead. But, in our present situation, at least five chil-
> dren in six who are born, lie a dead weight upon us, for want of
> employment. And a very skilful computer assured me, that above

*Reprinted from *Modern Philology,* XL (November, 1942), 161–170, by permission of the author and of the University of Chicago Press. Copyright 1942 by the
University of Chicago.

[1] *The prose works of Jonathan Swift, D.D.,* ed. Temple Scott (London, 1897-
1908), VII, 65. This edition will hereafter be referred to as *Works.*

one half of the souls in this kingdom supported themselves by begging and thievery; whereof two thirds would be able to get their bread in any other country upon earth. Trade is the only incitement to labour; where that fails the poor native must either beg, steal, or starve, or be forced to quit his country. This hath made me often wish, for some years past, that instead of discouraging our people from seeking foreign soil, the public would rather pay for transporting all our unnecessary mortals. . . . .[2]

The parallelism in ideas between this passage and *A modest proposal* is striking. In each there is the complaint that the people, for want of employment, must turn to begging and thievery, that a portion of the population is a useless burden, and that under certain conditions these/162/useless people could become a source of wealth to the nation. The ironic solution for Ireland's economic difficulties in each instance is the selling-off of human bodies, as slaves in the one case and as food in the other. In effect, Swift is maintaining that the maxim —people are the riches of a nation—applies to Ireland only if Ireland is permitted slavery or cannibalism. In both the *Maxims controlled in Ireland* and *A modest proposal* populousness is overtly and impliedly made a vicious economic condition for Ireland. The methods are, of course, different in the two, with *A modest proposal* gaining its effects through broad and sustained irony; but for fear that the reader may miss his telling point, that people are not the riches of Ireland whatever they may be in other countries, Swift inserts at the close of *A modest proposal* a more direct statement of his purpose:

I can think of no one objection, that will possibly be raised against this proposal, unless it should be urged that the number of people will be thereby much lessened in the kingdom. This I freely own, and was indeed one principal design in offering it to the world. I desire the reader will observe, that I calculate my remedy *for this one individual Kingdom of Ireland, and for no other that ever was, is, or, I think, ever can be upon earth.*[3]

The satirical point of *A modest proposal* would have been sharpened for Swift's contemporaries to the extent to which they believed the maxim it refuted. How much more damaging to England that her drastic policies had forced Ireland outside the pale in which universally valid economic laws could operate!

An examination of economic tracts in the second half of the seven-

---

[2] *Ibid.*, p. 70.
[3] *Ibid.*, pp. 214–15.

teenth century reveals constant iteration of the principle that people are the riches of a nation. Sir William Petty, whose views of Ireland were widely quoted in Swift's day, wrote that "Fewness of People is real poverty; and a Nation wherein are Eight Millions of People, are more than twice as rich as the same scope of Land wherein are but Four."[4] People, wrote William Petty, the supposed author of *Britannia languens* (1680), are "in truth the chiefest, most fundamental, and precious commodity."[5] Sir Josiah Child, great merchant and expound-/163/er of mercantilist ideas, maintained that "most Nations in the Civilized Parts of the World, are more or less Rich or Poor proportionably to the Paucity or Plenty of their People, and not to the Sterility or Fruitfulness of their Lands."[6] These statements are frequently repeated in the early eighteenth century. In *New essays on trade* (1702), Sir Francis Brewster wrote: "Nothing makes Kingdoms and Commonwealths, Mighty, Opulent and Rich, but multitudes of People; 'tis Crowds bring in Industry."[7] From Defoe came a similar expression: ". . . . the glory, the strength, the riches, the trade, and all that is valuable in a nation as to its figure in the world, depends upon the number of its people, be they never so mean and poor. . . . ."[8] These are typical expressions and could be multiplied. In their context and with their supporting arguments, these expressions, it is true, are not tantamount to an unqualified assertion that people are the riches of a nation. People are conceived of as a source of riches; their labor is potential wealth but it must be utilized. As one writer expressed it, the people are *"capital material . . . . raw* and indigested."[9]

Yet often the maxim was stated without qualification or without any attempt to equate the number of people and the employment available to them, although there was likely to be an assumption that employment could be provided.[10] The mercantilist wanted a large or

---

[4] *A treatise of taxes and contributions,* in *The economic writings of Sir William Petty,* ed. Charles H. Hull (Cambridge, 1899), I, 34.

[5] Reprinted in *A select collection of early English tracts on commerce,* ed. J. R. McCulloch (London, 1856), p. 458.

[6] *A new discourse of trade* (London, 1698), p. 179.

[7] P. 51.

[8] *Giving alms no charity* (1704); reprinted in *A collection of pamphlets concerning the poor,* ed. Thomas Gilbert (London, 1787), p. 71.

[9] William Petty, *Britannia languens,* in *A select collection . . . . ,* ed. McCulloch, p. 458.

[10] See the discussion on this point in Eli F. Heckscher, *Mercantilism,* trans. Mendel Shapiro (London, 1935), II, 159 ff. Heckscher writes: "It is natural to wonder how the notion that there could never be too great a population could ever be reconciled with the anxiety concerning the insufficiency of employment. In actual fact, this contradiction was never resolved."

dense population in order to keep wages low[11] and manufactures cheap, a condition by which a country gained an advantage in export trade, the great desideratum of the mercantilist. As William Petty wrote: "The *odds in Populacy* must also produce the like odds in Manufac-/164/ture; plenty of people must also cause *cheapness of wages:* which will cause cheapnesse of the Manufacture; in a scarcity of people wages must be dearer, which must cause the dearnesse of the Manufacture. . . . ."[12] Mandeville was thinking in the same terms when he declared that "in a free Nation where Slaves are not allow'd of, the surest Wealth consists in a Multitude of laborious Poor."[13] Though the insistence on populousness received support from serious economic writers by serious arguments, the maxim was as likely as not to be set down in nontechnical and popular writings without consideration of the implications and assumptions involved, as it was, for example, in the *Weekly journal, or Saturday's post,* April 11, 1724, and in the Irish weekly, the *Tribune,* No. 17 (1729).

Against the uncritical enunciation of the maxim there were sporadic protests. In an *Essay upon the probable methods of making a people gainer in the ballance of trade* (1699), Charles Davenant declared: "Their's is a wrong Opinion who think all Mouths profit a Country that consume its Product; And it may more truthfully be affirmed, That he who does not some way serve the Commonwealth, either by being employed, or by employing Others, is not only a useless, but a hurtful member to it."[14] A similar protest came from Laurence Braddon in 1723:

> But tho' *Populousness be designed as the greatest Blessing to a Nation, yet,* in fact, *it proves a Blessing only to that Kingdom and State,* where due care is taken . . . . *that* none, who are willing to work, shall be forced to be Idle for want of Employment. . . . . And where none who are able are permitted to live idle, by begging, or other more Vicious Practices. . . . .[15]

Swift, too, made a protest of the same nature. In *The history of the*

---

[11] See Jacob Viner, *Studies in the theory of international trade* (New York and London, 1937), pp. 56–57, where it is pointed out that commentators on mercantilism have neglected to take sufficiently into account dissent—on economic and humanitarian grounds—from the dominant doctrine that low wages are desirable. Viner's first two chapters, with their clear exposition of seventeenth- and eighteenth-century economic theory and their rich documentation from writers in the period, are of great value to the student of the history of ideas.

[12] *Britannia languens,* in *A select collection* . . . . , p. 349.

[13] *The fable of the bees,* ed. F. B. Kaye (Oxford, 1924), I, 287.

[14] P. 51.

[15] *To pay old debts without new taxes* (London, 1723), p. xi.

four last years of the queen, which he was writing in the trying days
near the end of Anne's reign, he complained that "The maxim, 'That
people are the riches of a nation,' hath been crudely understood by
many writers and reasoners upon that subject." At the moment his
animus was directed against the Palatines, whose numbers immigrat-
ing into England had increased the population by just so many dissenters; yet he was also establishing a general point: that populousness
per se is/165/not a blessing; that a person who does not function
productively in economic or political society makes the nation poorer,
not richer; and that such a person is comparable, to use Swift's own
figure, to a wen, which, although it makes a man fatter, is "unsightly
and troublesome, at best, and intercepts that nourishment, which
would otherwise diffuse itself through the whole body."[16]

Viewed against this background, *A modest proposal* is seen to be
another protest, in Swift's unique manner, against the unqualified
maxim that people are the riches of a nation. The tract was written
for a public in whose consciousness the maxim was firmly implanted,
in the expectation that the ironic impact would thus be greater. The
terrible irony in the bare maxim, divested of its supporting arguments,
was even more apparent at this time than usual because of the famine
conditions which prevailed in Ireland after three successive failures in
harvests; and Swift takes occasion in two other tracts, one written in
1728 and one in 1729, to insist that "the uncontrolled maxim, 'That
people are the riches of a Nation,' is no maxim here under our circumstances."[17] Here, at least, was one country where populousness was
not a virtue. Swift seemed to be aware—the evidence was before his
eyes—of the contradiction in the mercantilist attitude that the wealth
of a country was based on the poverty of the majority of its subjects.
However, we must guard against endowing Swift with unusual knowledge of or insight into economic matters,[18] or even seeing him as moving against the trend of mercantilist thought. His purpose was not
primarily to expose an economic fallacy; it was purely propagandistic:

---

[16] *Works,* X, 114–15.

[17] *Ibid.,* VII, 114, 139.

[18] There is no evidence that Swift did any extended or systematic reading in
economic theory. His library contained the following: Josiah Child, *Discourse on
trade* (1693); Charles Davenant, *Picture of a modern whig: with other tracts*
(1701); John Browne, *Essays on the trade and coin of Ireland* (1729); John Locke,
Tracts relating to money, interest and trade (1696); William Petty, *Essays in political arithmetick* (1699); Samuel Madden, *Reflections and resolutions for the gentlemen of Ireland* (1738). I have listed these in the order in which they appear in the
Sales Catalogue reprinted by Harold Williams in *Dean Swift's library* (Cambridge,
1932), Nos. 276, 288, 300, 412, 435, 444. To these may be added the economic tracts
of Sir William Temple

to put the onus on England of vitiating the working of natural economic law in Ireland by denying Irishmen "the same natural rights common to the rest of mankind."

It would seem, on merely logical grounds, that Swift should have favored a reduction of the population to achieve a higher level of sub-/166/sistence, that he should have defended, for example, the emigration of the Irish people to the American colonies; and he did pretend to see in emigration a partial solution. In *Maxims controlled in Ireland* he wrote that he has often wished "for some years past, that instead of discouraging our people from seeking foreign soil, the public would rather pay for transporting all our unnecessary mortals, whether Papists or Protestants, to America."[19] He repeats the view in the *Intelligencer*, No. 19: "It must needs be a very comfortable circumstance, in the present juncture, that some thousand families are gone, or going, or preparing to go, from hence, and settle themselves in America."[20] But these statements, viewed in their context, are seen to be ironic, their function being to emphasize the dire position of a country which must resort to emigration. In the light of contemporary economic theory, with its insistence on an increasing population, emigration could not be viewed with complacency; it was not acceptable as a solution. There was much concern that England's population was declining or was not increasing at a sufficiently rapid rate; and many mercantilists advocated encouragements to marriage, to achieve a higher birth rate,[21] and laws to facilitate immigration.[22] There were

---

[19] *Works*, VII, 70.

[20] *Ibid.*, IX, 328.

[21] In *A modest proposal* Swift lists among the ironical advantages of his proposal that it "would be a great inducement to marriage, which all wise nations have either encouraged by rewards, or enforced by laws and penalties" (*Works*, VII, 214). Charles Davenant complained that the duties imposed on marriages and birth were detrimental: "a very grievous Burthen upon the poorer Sort, whose Numbers compose the Strength and Wealth of any Nation." He adds: "In order to have Hands to carry on Labour and Manufactures, which must make us Gainers in the Ballance of Trade, we ought not to deterr but rather invite Men to marry . . . ." (*An essay upon the probable methods of making a people gainers in the ballance of trade* [London, 1699], p. 33). Contrast Swift's statement in *A proposal for giving badges to the beggars of Dublin* (1737): "As this is the only Christian country where people contrary to the old maxim, are the poverty and not the riches of the nation, so, the blessing of increase and multiply is by us converted into a curse: and, as marriage hath been ever countenanced in all free countries, so we should be less miserable if it were discouraged in ours, as far as can be consistent with Christianity" (*Works*, VII, 330).

[22] In *The history of the four last years of the queen*, Swift makes an interesting application of the maxim, that people are the riches of a nation, to the problem of immigration (*Works*, X, 114–15). On the immigration and naturalization of foreigners see Slingsby Bethel, *An account of the French usurpation upon the trade of England* (London, 1679), p. 15; Charles Davenant, *Discourses on the public revenues and trade of England* (London, 1698), II, 199; William Wood, *A survey of trade* (London, 1718), pp. 299 ff.

complaints that emigration to the colonies has been detrimental to the nation. "The peopling of the American Plantations subject to the Crown of England," wrote Roger Coke, "hath diminished the strength of Eng-/167/land."[23] It is not, Slingsby Bethel maintained, in "the interest of State, to suffer such multitudes of people to pass out of his Majesties Kingdoms into other Princes Dominions, or the Western Plantations, thereby to disfurnish our selves of people; the sad consequences and effects whereof, are too visible in the misfortunes of *Spain*."[24] The author of *Britannia languens* argued in the same vein: ". . . . our *Plantation-Trade* hath robbed and prevented us of some Millions of our People, amongst which very many being, or might have been Manufacturers, the Nation hath also lost more Millions of Pounds in the loss of their Manufactures."[25] Those Irishmen, Swift among them,[26] who had observed the losses to Ireland resulting from the emigration of workers in the Irish woolen industry to France, Spain, Germany, and the Low Countries—an exodus caused by the restrictive acts passed by the English Parliament at the close of the seventeenth century—would have read such complaints understandingly.

Many mercantilists found, however, that they could reconcile emigration to colonies with the desire for an increasing population and the fear of loss of numbers. It could not be denied that by reducing the number of laborers in the nation emigration tended to raise the costs of labor and manufactures and thus to put the country in a less favorable position for advantageous foreign trade; yet it could be and was argued that colonies compensated for the disadvantages created by providing raw materials to be manufactured in the mother-country and a market for the finished products. Emigration to colonies whose trade was carefully controlled by navigation acts was justifiable, therefore, if such colonies created employment at home and swelled the exports to a value greater than that lost by the numbers who emigrated. Thus Sir Josiah Child wrote: "That all Colonies and foreign Plantations do endamage their Mother-Kingdom, whereof the Trades (of such Plantations) are not confined to their said Mother-Kingdom, by good Laws and severe Execution of those Laws."[27] He continued: /168/

---

[23] *A treatise wherein is demonstrated that the church and state of England are in equal danger with the trade of it* (London, 1671), p. 26.

[24] *An account of the French usurpation upon the trade of England* (London, 1679), p. 16.

[25] P. 370.

[26] Any reader of the Irish tracts will recall examples of Swift's laments about the Irish woolen industry.

[27] P. 194.

Plantations being at first furnished, and afterwards successively supplied with People from their Mother-Kingdoms, and People being Riches, that loss of People to the Mother-Kingdoms, be it more or less, is certainly a damage, except the employment of those People abroad, do cause the employment of so many more at home in their Mother-Kingdoms. . . . [28]

The argument is more fully expressed by John Cary:

. . . . it having been a great question among many thoughtful Men whether our Foreign Plantations have been an advantage to this Nation, the reasons they give against them are, that they have drained us of Multitudes of our People who might have been serviceable at home and advanced Improvements in Husbandry and Manufacture; That the Kingdom of *England* is worse Peopled by so much as they are increased; and that Inhabitants being the Wealth of a Nation, by how much they are lessened, by so much we are poorer than when we first began to settle our Foreign Colonies; Though I allow the last Proposition to be true, that People are or may be made the Wealth of a Nation . . . . Its my Opinion that our Plantations are an Advantage . . . . every one more or less, as they take off our Product and Manufactures, supply us with Commodities which may be either wrought up here, or Exported again, or prevent fetching things of the same Nature from other Princes for our home Consumption, imploy our Poor, and encourage our Navigation. . . . . [29]

Such justifications, as Swift was aware, had no application to Ireland, which was itself treated as a colony, with its trade strictly controlled by the Navigation Acts in the interests of England. An emigrant from England, Holland, or France might be looked upon as a unit of economic value who would eventually return his value to the mother-country; but one could hardly apply the same economic logic to the Irish emigrant, whose country was peculiarly removed from the operations of economic law. "I have often taken notice," Swift wrote, "both in print and in discourse, that there is no topic so fallacious . . . . as to argue how we ought to act in Ireland, from the example of England, Holland, France, or any other country, whose inhabitants are allowed the common rights and liberties of humankind." [30] Public-spirited Irishmen were concerned at the numbers who were departing. Even Lord Primate Boulter, whose first thought was for the welfare of

---

[28] *Ibid.*, p. 195.
[29] *An essay on the state of England, in relation to its trade, its poor, and its taxes* (Bristol, 1695), pp. 65–66.
[30] *Works*, VII, 196; see also VII, 66, 123, 339.

England rather than for Ireland, was disturbed in 1728, when/169/
famine was widespread, at the size of the emigration. In a letter written to the Duke of Newcastle, then Secretary of State, Boulter brought
the problem before the English Cabinet for possible parliamentary
action:

> I am very sorry I am obliged to give your Grace so melancholy
> an account of the state of this kingdom. . . . . For we have had
> three bad harvests together there [in the north], which has made
> oatmeal, which is their great subsistence, much dearer than ordi-
> nary. . . . . We have had for several years some agents from the
> colonies in *America*, and several masters of ships that have gone
> about the country, and deluded the people with stories of great
> plenty and estates to be had for going for in those parts of the
> world: and they have been better able to seduce people, by reason
> of the necessities of the poor so late. . . . . But whatever occasions
> their going, it is certain that above 4,200 men, women, and chil-
> dren have been shipped off from hence for the *West Indies* within
> three years, and of these above 3,100 this last summer. . . . . The
> whole north is in a ferment at present, and people every day en-
> gaging one another to go next year to the *West Indies*. The hu-
> mour has spread like a contagious distemper, and the people will
> hardly hear any body that tries to cure them of their madness.[31]

Swift, too, was genuinely perturbed. In 1728 and 1729 he refers
several times to the subject of emigrating Irishmen, particularly to
those who are leaving for America, which for several reasons he thinks
no better than Ireland. Like Boulter, he believed that they had been
given false representations and that they were doomed to disappoint-
ment; yet he is not at a loss to understand their motives for going,
since "men in the extremest degree of misery, and want, will naturally
fly to the first appearance of relief, let it be ever so vain, or visionary."[32] It was at this time that Swift wrote *A modest proposal* and its
lesser known companion piece, *An answer to the craftsman*. This last
tract was occasioned by the license given to France to recruit Irishmen
for military service in the French army; and it too is a bitter and ironic
commentary, among other matters, on the subject of Ireland's depopulation by England. As he had done in *A modest proposal*, Swift makes
in this tract an ironical computation of the monetary profit to Ireland
from the reduction and destruction of its people. And he adds this recommendation: ". . . . for fear of increasing the natives in this/170/

---

[31] *Letters written by His Excellency Hugh Boulter . . . . to several ministers of state in England* (Dublin, 1770), I, 209–10.
[32] *Works*, IX, 330; see also VII, 120, 123.

island, that an annual draught, according to the number born every year, be exported to whatever prince will bear the carriage, or transplanted to the English dominions on the American continent, as a screen between his Majesty's English subjects and the savage Indians."[33]

What Swift wanted for Ireland was not fewer people but more opportunities—opportunities that would present themselves if England adopted a less restrictive policy, if the Irish absentees were regulated, and if the Irish people could be made to see wherein their welfare lay. He maintained, as did many contemporary Irishmen,[34] that Ireland possessed the potentialities of a rich country and could, under proper conditions, easily support its population. Ireland, he wrote, "is the poorest of all civilized countries in Europe, with every natural advantage to make it one of the richest."

---

[33] *Ibid.*, VII, 222. Compare this passage with what Swift has to say in the *Intelligencer*, No. 19, on the conditions which confront the Irish emigrant to America: "The English established in those colonies, are in great want of men to inhabit that tract of ground, which lies between them, and the wild Indians who are not reduced under their dominion. We read of some barbarous people, whom the Romans placed in their armies, for no other service, than to blunt their enemies' swords, and afterward to fill up trenches with their dead bodies. And thus our people who transport themselves, are settled in those interjacent tracts, as a screen against the insults of the savages, and may have as much land, as they can clear from the woods, at a very reasonable rate, if they can afford to pay about a hundred years' purchase by their labour" (*Works*, IX, 329–30).

[34] Cf. John Browne, *An essay on trade in general, and on that of Ireland in particular* (Dublin, 1728), pp. 38–39; George Berkeley, *The querist* (1735), Nos. 123–24, 132–34, 272–73; *Some thoughts on the tillage of Ireland* (Dublin, 1738), pp. 52 f.

Martin Price

From Swift's Rhetorical Art: A Study in Structure and Meaning*

In *A Modest Proposal* Swift achieves the most economical and intense use of the ironic mask. The apparent author is an ingenious projector attempting what no one before has achieved, a reconciliation of England's interest with Ireland's and a demonstration that in Ireland, as well as in other lands, people are the riches of a nation. Recent scholars have shown that the Modest Proposer is not only a typical projector but, more important, a typical theorist of a certain kind, the political arithmetician. The burden of the satire may be taken to rest upon the economic theorists of the day—men like Petty, Petyt, Child, Brewster, and Defoe—or upon the conditions which make their theories inapplicable to Ireland.

In effect, Swift is maintaining that the maxim—people are the riches of a nation—applies to Ireland only if Ireland is permitted slavery or cannibalism. . . . The terrible irony in the bare maxim, divested of its supporting arguments, was even more apparent at this time than usual because of the famine conditions which prevailed in Ireland after three successive failures in harvests.[1]

*Reprinted from Martin Price, *Swift's Rhetorical Art: A Study in Structure and Meaning* (New Haven: Yale University Press, 1953), pp. 71–74, by permission of the author and publisher. Copyright 1953 by the Yale University Press.

[1] Louis A. Landa, *"A Modest Proposal* and Populousness," *Modern Philology*, 40 (1942), 162, 165. See also George Wittkowsky, "Swift's *Modest Proposal:* The Biography of an Early Georgian Pamphlet," *Journal of the History of Ideas*, 4 (1943), 65–104, esp. 94–5; Louis A. Landa, "Swift's Economic Views and Mercantilism," *ELH*, 10 (1943), 310–35; Cleanth Brooks, *Modern Poetry and the Tradition* (Chapel Hill, University of North Carolina Press, 1939), pp. 226–7.

What we have is a paradoxical application of the maxim to Ireland written in a style which betrays no awareness of the paradox and which resembles very closely the scientific manner of the economic projectors of the day.

As in the poetic fables or in Gulliver's initial account of the "very short and soft" grass of Lilliput, Swift prepares unobtrusively for the surprise which follows. The very first paragraph shows the displacement of tone which characterizes the author's insensibility:

> It is a melancholy object to those, who walk through this great town, or travel in the country, when they see the streets, the roads, and cabindoors, crowded with beggars of the female sex, followed by three, four, or six children, *all in rags,* and importuning every passenger for an alms. These mothers instead of being able to work for their honest livelihood, are forced to employ all their time in strolling, to beg sustenance/72/ for their helpless infants, who, as they grow up, either turn thieves for want of work, or leave their dear Native Country to fight for the Pretender in Spain, or sell themselves to the Barbadoes.[2]

There is a certain fastidious preciseness of phrase in this which belies the sympathy one might expect. The reaction of the author to the beggars is clearly that of the passing observer, and his profession of sentiment in "melancholy" is counteracted by the classificatory interest of "beggars of the female sex, followed by three, four, or six children." There is no necessary conflict between genuine compassion and preciseness of observation, the virtuoso in the world's laboratory. The strangeness of tone becomes more apparent when the "beggars of the female sex" become "mothers" but mothers whose children render them unable "to work for their honest livelihood." This view of motherhood is coupled with "helpless infants," a phrase which might render conventional pity but which here designates an encumbrance to respectable labor. Finally the slight incongruity of "this great town" gives emphasis to the later reference to a "dear Native Country" which children must desert in order to find a living. The play on the emptiness of stale terms is one of Swift's favorite entertainments. Here it is characterization of an author who lives by "refined jargon."

So far we may simply be disturbed by the author's ability to consider human misery in detached economic terms and still to retain

---

[2] TS, VII, 207.

the stereotypes of compassion and patriotism. In what follows, the zeal of a projector becomes apparent as well:

> whoever could find out a fair, cheap and easy method of making these children sound useful members of the commonwealth would deserve so well of the public, as to have his statue set up for a preserver of the nation.
>
> But my intention is very far from being confined to provide only for the children of professed beggars, it is of a much greater extent and shall take in the whole number of infants at a certain age, who are born of parents in effect as little able to support them, as those who demand our charity in the streets.[3]

This last sentence has a multiple function. It reflects the ambition of a projector who would outdo all rivals with a comprehensive plan when even a more moderate aim has not yet been satisfied. It points, also, to the full extent of Irish poverty: the cottagers no less than the beggars demand our charity. The plan must become the more extravagant to meet a problem so vast. The situation of Ireland (both in its poverty and in its subjection to England's mercantile colonial policy) is such that only a fool can hope to satisfy both justice and the English. The/73/ambition is another side of the obtuseness we have already seen. So far it is only foolish, but an ominous note is prepared in the phrasing: "sound useful members of the commonwealth," like "helpless infants" before, ironically foreshadows the proposal that is to be made. As usual, Swift is preparing his text to shift easily into a further level of meaning which will reverse the import of the whole tract.

Once the zeal of the projector is established, his moral nature is allowed to become more obvious. Mothers become "dams" and "breeders," children are "dropped." The Modest Proposer can mourn for "the poor innocent babes" murdered by their mothers; but he can look forward to making them "contribute to the feeding and partly to the clothing of many thousands." The intensity and obliviousness of his economic interest lead him to weigh the usefulness of children's proficiency in the art of theft. When the proposal is finally set forth, it is delicately qualified by a regard for refined modern tastes: "a young healthy child well nursed is at a year old a most delicious, nourishing, and wholesome food, whether stewed, roasted, baked, or boiled, *and I have no doubt that it will equally*

---

[3] TS, vii, 207–8.

serve in a fricassee or ragout".[4] The use of physical horror—the plan
for "buying the children alive, and dressing them hot under the
Knife"—has much the same function as the use of disgust in other
works. Just as man's pride in his rationality must be confronted with
a concrete image of his animal drives in the Yahoos, the benign theo-
rizers about economic man must be made to see their abstraction
come to life at the very moment when their inhumanity is most
flagrant. The concrete instance tests the theory: that it does not
destroy it for the Modest Proposer is due to his singular blindness.
That blindness, in turn, is only an exaggeration of a more common
indifference, the refusal or the inability to see the concrete and the
readiness to submit to noble pretensions.

The proposal is offered, not by an Englishman with the indifference of a superior foreigner but by an Irishman anxious to please
England, the kind of eager collaborator who can outdo the oppres-
sors. "Swift's anger was always divided between the stupidity of the
Irish and the rapacity of the English,"[5] but Irish stupidity could be
something worse: "there is not a more undeserving vicious race of
human kind than the bulk of those who are reduced to beggary,
even as this beggarly country."[6] It is Swift's ability to see the degradation, moral as well as economic, of the victims who submit to the
victors that gives universality to such a work as the *Modest Proposal*.
Swift lamented that in Ireland "the blessing of increase and multiply
is . . . converted into a curse: and, as marriage hath been ever
countenanced in all free countries, so we should be less miserable
if it were discouraged in ours, as far as can be/74/consistent with
Christianity."[7] In the modest proposal, marriage is made to prosper
by conforming with interest:

> This would be a great inducement to marriage, which all wise
> nations have either encouraged by rewards, or enforced by laws
> and penalties. It would increase the care and tenderness of
> mothers toward their children, when they are sure of a settle-
> ment for life, to the poor babes, provided in some sort by the
> public for their annual profit instead of expense. We should see
> an honest emulation among the married women, which of them
> could bring the fattest child to the market, men would become
> as fond of their wives during the time of their pregnancy, as they

---

[4] TS, vii, 209. Italics added.
[5] *The Drapier's Letters*, ed. Davis, introd., p. xi.
[6] *A Proposal for Giving Badges to the Beggars of Dublin*, TS, vii, 329–30.
[7] TS, vii, 330.

are now of their mares in foal, their cows in calf, or sows when they are ready to farrow, nor offer to beat or kick them (as is too frequent a practice) for fear of a miscarriage.[8]

There is more general irony in this passage than in most of the tract; not only is Ireland's plight underlined and the author's grossness further exposed, but a general tendency in all men is suggested. Decent human behavior is made possible only by the coincidental demands of interest. Proper family relations are possible only as the chance appearances of real selfishness. People do not serve God; they occasionally appear to do so when the worship of Mammon requires similar gestures. This goes beyond even La Rochefoucauld: there is no hypocrisy here, no homage paid virtue by vice, only the accident of resemblance. The Modest Proposer is rationalizing not merely England's oppression but man's universal lack of charity.

The same note is struck in the final sentence: "I have no children, by which I can propose to get a single penny; the youngest being nine years old, and my wife past childbearing."[9] We can see most clearly the reason for the theorizer's detachment: he is free of facing the concrete instance himself. That he is capable of considering it is damning enough, but more is suggested. The accusations he fends off are such as might be made when men once esteem children for their commercial value and their wives as the producers of commodities. The very fullness of meaning that Swift's irony suggests saves the tract from the flatness of propaganda; the Modest Proposer implicates more and more of us in his own madness. His obtuseness becomes the comic counterpart of a much more terrible moral degradation. This device is frequent in Swift: his patient fools are always less terrible than the knaves they betray. The surface of the irony is a comedy of irresponsible folly, of the moral obliviousness of a dedicated pedant or theorist. Beneath the surface lies the guilt of most men, who are less naive and transparent but all the more responsible.

---

[8] TS, VII, 214.
[9] TS, VII, 216.

J. W. Johnson

Tertullian and "A Modest Proposal"*

Although Jonathan Swift has been a prime object for source hunt-
ers almost since his own day, with the result that the *Tale of a Tub*
and *Gulliver's Travels* have been copiously annotated, there have
been almost no suggestions as to possible sources of influence on "A
Modest Proposal." Sir Walter Scott noted that in its recommendation of infant cannibalism as a solution to extreme poverty the
"Proposal" bore certain resemblances to a suggestion advanced during the time of the siege of Jerusalem.[1] Charles Townsend Copeland
suggested that legendary tales of the devouring of infants by the
Cavaliers during the Civil War, as well as a reference to *paidophagy*
in Act III of a play, the *Old Troop, or Monsieur Ragout,* may have
been known to Swift.[2] But it would appear that the most obvious and
direct influence on Swift's proposal, stylistically as well as themati-
cally, was the *Apologia* of Tertullian.

Tertullian's *Apology*, a defense of Christianity notable for its
acerb and honed style, was a work with which Swift was familiar
and of which he was apparently quite fond. As early as the 1690's,
Swift/562/was making abstracts of Tertullian and other church
fathers at Moor Park; and at the time of his death in Dublin in 1745,
he still retained an edition of Tertullian's works in his library.[3] The

---

*Reprinted from *Modern Language Notes*, LXXIII (December, 1958), 561–563,
by permission of the author and the publisher. Copyright 1958 by The Johns
Hopkins Press.
[1] Sir Walter Scott, ed., *The Works of Jonathan Swift* (London, 1883), I, 341.
[2] Charles Townsend Copeland, "On Dean Swift's 'A Modest Proposal'," in *The
Harvard Advocate Anthology*, ed. Donald Hall (New York, 1950), pp. 46–49.
[3] Cf. Edward Bensley, "The Library at Moor Park," N & Q, CLIX (1930), 48;
Harold Williams, *Dean Swift's Library, With a Facsimile of the Original Sales
Catalogue* (Cambridge, England, 1932).

most obvious testament to Swift's affinity to Tertullian, however, lies in the striking structural and stylistic parallels between the *Apology* and "A Modest Proposal."

Tertullian's defense of Christianity was undertaken because of the persecution of Christian converts by the Romans on the grounds that the religious sect was engaging in inhuman practices and that its adherents were, therefore, not to be treated as human beings. The exact nature of the charges of animalism against the Christians is first disclosed when Tertullian ironically exclaims that Roman officials had undertaken a fruitless investigation to discover "how many murdered babies each of us [Christians] has tasted"; then he scathingly remarks, "Oh! The glory of that magistrate who had brought to light some Christian who had eaten up to date a hundred babies!"[4]

Having established the idea of cannibalism and postulated the attitude of a Roman "projector," Tertullian goes on in the best Swiftian fashion to identify himself with the projector's point of view and carry it to its logical conclusion. Very well then, he declares, let us accept the absurd premise that the Christians ceremonially eat children and reconstruct the process. First the Christian initiate must approach the "father" of the ritual to make preparations, who would instruct him as follows: " . . . you must have a baby, still tender, that can know nothing of death, that can smile under your knife; *item,* a loaf, to catch its juicy blood. . . ."[5] Tertullian envisions the actual ceremony in all its grisly horror: "Come! Plunge the knife into the baby, nobody's enemy, guilty of nothing, everybody's child; or if that is the other man's job , do you just stand by (that is all), by this human creature dying before it has lived; watch for the young soul as it escapes; catch the infant blood; steep your bread with it; eat and enjoy it."[6]

Having scored his point, Tertullian underlines it by substituting his own premise in place of the false one that Christians are subhuman: "You, sir, who cannot do the thing [i.e., eat children] ought/563/not to believe it of another. For a Christian too is a man, and exactly what you are."[7] Yet human depravity is such that men will attempt to justify their own cruelty toward other men by accusing their victims of being lower than human: "Man's flesh goes belching, fattened on man's flesh."[8]

---

[4] Tertullian, *Apology*, Loeb ed. (London, 1931), II. 5.
[5] VIII. 7.
[6] VIII. 1–2.
[7] VIII. 5.
[8] IX. 11.

When he contemplated the Anglo-Irish situation in the 1720's, Swift found much that could remind him of the persecution of the Christians by the Roman officials. A minority was being victimized by a group that held economic and governmental control over them on the grounds that they were little more than animals. Very well, declares Swift, grant that the Irish are "dams" and "breeders," the projector is then free to follow his premise to its logical conclusion. Swift's matter of fact tone parallels Tertullian's: in the factual proposal, in the itemized calculations regarding price; in the same hideously violent account of the butchering of the children. And there is the same dreadful discussion, carried on in the most acidly serene tone, about the actual eating of the baby, though the refinements of cooking and seasoning are Swift's own.[9]

It has been said of the *Apology*, "As an argument, it is magnificent; and Tertullian's command of sarcasm is unsurpassed in history. But this is defiance, not persuasion; bitter satire, not gentle pleading. . . ."[10] With the qualification that Tertullian's sarcasm has been at least equalled by Swift, we may accept the rest of the evaluation as being also true of "A Modest Proposal."

---

[9] Jonathan Swift, "A Modest Proposal," in *The Prose Works of Jonathan Swift*, ed. Herbert Davis (Oxford, 1955), XII, 110–116, *et passim*.

[10] Henry M. Gwatkin, quoted in *Apology*, p. xix.

Edward W. Rosenheim, Jr.

From Swift and the Satirist's Art*

Strangely enough, *A Modest Proposal*[1] presents the reader with some of the same difficulties that are encountered in the *Argument.* /47/With the exception of *Gulliver's Travels,* Swift's grotesque argument for infant cannibalism as a solution to the problems of Ireland is certainly the most widely read of his works. And it may be argued that the ordinary reader has little difficulty in understanding *A Modest Proposal* or in responding with shocked fascination to the incomparably outrageous method by which Swift suggests that a tragic human problem be overcome.

In subsequent discussion, we shall note the importance of Swift's uniquely memorable fiction, in itself, as a source of the appeal which *A Modest Proposal* has retained through the centuries. For the moment, however, let us concern ourselves with the work as a satiric attack and again raise the question which is primary for the analysis of satire. What is the object of Swift's attack in this famous document?

It may, of course, be argued that Swift's chief purpose is to reveal, in the most arresting possible terms, the full horror of the Irish economic situation. And certainly this is one of the achievements of the tract since, in effect, the "proposer" adopts a posture in which he implies that cannibalism is a reasonable alternative to an unspeakable status quo. When, however, we assert that the chief effect of the

---

* This portion is reprinted from *Swift and the Satirist's Art* by Edward W. Rosenheim, Jr., by permission of the University of Chicago Press. Copyrighted 1963 by the University of Chicago. All rights reserved. Published 1963. Reprinted also by permission of the author.

[1] Textual references to *A Modest Proposal* can be found in *Prose Works,* XII, 107-18.

tract is to underscore the lamentable condition of the Irish peasantry, we court difficulties. It is true that, as a preliminary to the
proposal itself, Swift is able to provide an appalling—and, one
judges, not excessively distorted — view of the hopeless squalor
and suffering which afflict his countrymen. Yet how does the "proposal" itself serve to reinforce this distressing picture? The answer
one is tempted to give is that the proposal is no more shocking than
the state of affairs which actually exists. Yet this implies that the
proposal is therefore authentic, that the document is an affirmative,
literal argument, that we are to take the author's position seriously—
and that, in short, we are dealing not with satire but with a straightforward advocacy of the most revolting economic project ever to
occur to a Western mind.

That such an interpretation is unthinkable need not, I hope, be
argued. It is clear, from the scrutiny of all that has been written
about *A Modest Proposal*, that thoughtful readers of the tract refuse
to accept its argument literally, seek beyond Swift's apparent attitude
for some essential object of attack, and, in effect, regard the work as
satiric in substantially the terms which we have been employing to
define this species of writing. Such responses have led to a number
/48/of illuminating suggestions concerning the true direction which
is taken by the work. One of the most common conclusions to be
offered is that the ultimate object of satiric attack is the English—
and sometimes more specifically, English legislators, landlords, or
economic apologies. From such an approach, Swift's *persona* can be
seen—as he is in the *Argument*—to represent his satiric victim; the
extravagant inhumanity of his proposal is thus construed as a distortion (or perhaps merely a *reductio ad absurdum*) of English indifference to the most basic matters of human need when they are
manifested in Ireland. The acceptance of such an interpretation,
however, is difficult for several reasons. The *persona* is not identified
in any way with a position that might be characteristic of the English. Indeed, throughout the text he is clearly addressing his Irish
countrymen and regards the nation as his own.[2] Moreover, we have,
in the *Drapier's Letters* and elsewhere, abundant evidence of the
kind of viciousness in practice and policy with which Swift is willing
to tax the English nation; in *A Modest Proposal*, however, we
are allowed to see, at most, the consequences of English evil, and it

---

[2] E.g., "this great Town" (p. 109); "For we can neither employ them..."
(p. 110); "this one individual Kingdom of Ireland" (p. 116); "by advancing our
Trade" (p. 118).

is Irish policy, or lack thereof, in the face of these consequences which occupies the writer.

Efforts to locate the object of satiric attack with greater precision have also led to the view that the *Modest Proposal* is largely a parody or derisive caricature of writings which have preceded it. And certainly in the glib and pseudo-systematic working-out of particulars and anticipation of objections there are mocking echoes of what must have been familiar discussions of Irish problems.[3] There is likewise, without doubt, a derisive distortion of influential economic theories, particularly, as Professor Landa has pointed out, those of the mercantilists.[4] The question remains, however, whether the/49/ bleak clarity with which the Irish plight is represented, the savage resentment which it has engendered, and the repellant solution which is offered can be satisfactorily explained as assaults upon either the substance or the language of previously published attempts to deal with the problems of the Irish.

As is so often true in Swift's satire, there are several victims against whom, by a single comprehensive satiric fiction, appropriate thrusts are delivered. But at the same time, only one end can account for all of the means which the writer has employed in the *Modest Proposal,* and one candidate alone qualifies as the principal goal of Swift's attack. The central satiric victim in this tract, as in the *Argument against Abolishing Christianity,* is the audience for whom the work is primarily intended. The audience—and satiric target—are the Irish people themselves; or, more explicitly, that part of the people of Ireland which determines the country's policies. Swift here is again the angry preacher, bent upon the exposure of the lethargy and obtuseness of his congregation. The "melancholly Object" which is the spectacle of Irish poverty is, after all, the occasion for the

---

[3] See Davis' Introduction, *Prose Works,* XII, xx-xxi.

[4] *A Modest Proposal* and Populousness," *Modern Philology,* XL (1942), 161-70, and "Swift's Economic Views and Mercantilism," *ELH,* X (1943), 310-35. See also George Wittkowsky, "Swift's *Modest Proposal:* The Biography of an Early Georgian Pamphlet," *Journal of the History of Ideas,* IV (1943), 75-104. Wittkowsky points to rather clear analogies between Swift's style and putative purpose and the writings of those economic projectors who practiced "political arithmetic"; his case might, indeed, have been strengthened by noting the association of such a founder of the new economic science as Sir William Petty with the Royal Society (and particularly its Irish correspondents) during the period (1682-85) when the *Philosophical Transactions* furnished abundant material for Swift's future attacks on the projectors. To imply, however, that even "from the point of view of the student of political economy" (p. 104) the tract is a parody of mercantilist theories, is to ignore the facts—largely economic—of Irish, wretchedness and apathy which, in 1729, were Swift's most passionate concern.

tract, but the plain facts about Irish populousness must have been lamentably familiar to Swift's original readers. The elaborate, systematic advocacy of the proposal, with its resemblance to the manner in which other "projects" have been couched, strikes passing satiric blows at victims ranging from absentee Anglo-Irish Protestants to the prolific Irish peasantry. But the crucial impact of the satire becomes unmistakable only belatedly, in the famous passage which asserts that this remedy is calculated "for this one individual Kingdom of IRELAND, and for no other that ever was, is, or I think ever can be upon Earth."

> Therefore, [*Swift goes on*] let no man talk to me of other Expedients: *of taxing our Absentees at five Shillings a Pound: of using neither Cloaths, nor Household Furniture except what is of our own Growth and Manufacture: Of utterly rejecting the Materials and Instruments that promote*/50/*foreign luxury: Of curing the Expensiveness of Pride, Vanity, Idleness, and Gaming in our Women: Of introducing a Vein of Parsimony, Prudence and Temperance: Of learning to love our Country, wherein we differ even from LAPLANDERS, and the Inhabitants of TOPINAMBOO: Of quitting our Animosities, and Factions; nor act any longer like the* Jews, *who were murdering one another at the very Moment their City was taken: Of being a little cautious not to sell our Country and Consciences for nothing: Of teaching Landlords to have, at least, one Degree of Mercy towards their Tenants.* Lastly, *Of putting a Spirit of Honesty, Industry, and Skill into our Shop-keepers; who, if a Resolution could now be taken to buy only our native Goods, would immediately unite to cheat and exact upon us in the Price, the Measure, and the Goodness; nor could ever yet be brought to make one fair Proposal of just Dealing, though often and earnestly invited to it* (pp. 116-17).

What is immediately clear about these "other Expedients" is that they represent the precise steps which Swift has long advocated.[5] And when this fact is recognized, the entire context of the *Modest Proposal* becomes clear. Writing to Pope in the year previous to the publication of this tract, Swift denies all motives of disinterested altruism in his concern for Irish affairs. "I do profess," he says, "without affectation, that your kind opinion of me as a patriot, since you call it so, is what I do not deserve; because what I do is owing

---

[5] See earlier "Irish Tracts" in *Prose Works*, XII, 1-90 *passim*, including *Intelligencer*, No. 19 (pp. 54-61).

to perfect rage and resentment, and the mortifying sight of slavery, folly, and baseness about me, among which I am forced to live."[6]

In the light of this kind of statement, *A Modest Proposal* is very close to a direct expression of Swift's rage and disgust, and the *persona*, driven by the obdurate rejection of every reasonable "other expedient" into the advocacy of a final, outrageous solution, is not very different from the historic figure of the bitterly frustrated Dean of St. Patrick's.

We are bound to discover in this document the sort of conceit which, for many readers, is memorable because of its unique Swiftian amalgam of wild fancy and perverse logic. We likewise recognize a variety of satiric assaults which find their mark in such diversified phenomena as anti-Catholicism, sexual irregularity, the follies of people of fashion, and, as we have suggested, most notably the/51/ economic projectors, among them those who had offered prescriptions for Irish problems. The principal satiric achievement, however, must be seen as persuasive and, indeed, once more a "homiletic" one. Swift is concerned with providing, for an audience whom he regards as lethargic and foolish, the most devastating assessment of their own condition and with arguing, almost literally, that as they have rejected all reasonable courses of action, the incredibly repellent proposal he advances is at least better than doing nothing.

This is, in truth, an address to and an assault upon "this one individual Kingdom of Ireland," for, whatever Swift may have felt about the English conduct of Irish affairs, within this document it is the Irish who are plainly taxed with bringing about their own deplorable condition. The so-called "paradox" of Swift's furious nationalism is illuminated rather than complicated by *A Modest Proposal*. For a people who should, he believes, truthfully "think it a great happiness to have been sold for Food at a Year old," Swift offers, in his anger, a prescription for virtual race suicide which is no more shocking than the state of affairs at which, through the folly of their own national policy, they have already arrived.

---

[6] *Correspondence*, IV, 34.

Maurice Johnson

The Structural Impact of
*A Modest Proposal**

A Modest Proposal (1729) has been singled out as the one incontestable example of poetic passion in English Augustan literature. Its pervasive irony, metaphorical contrasts, and paradox have been described as operating on a "grander scale than in any poem of its day." Simultaneously, it has been studied as an early Georgian tract dealing with contemporary mercantilist attitudes toward balance of trade, economic statism, Irish absentee landlords, English policy, the impotent poor, and theories of population. *A Modest Proposal* is currently employed to illustrate a single department of Jonathan Swift's rhetorical art: his feigning an alien identity and situation, acting in character to achieve his satire. In the universities the present idea of Swift is that of The Man in the Ironic Mask.[1]

Yet these varied studies do not explain the effect made by *A Modest Proposal*. I suppose that the total impact of the essay — felt in the reading like an electric charge — cannot be satisfactorily assessed. (There is nothing else like it in literature, said Taine.) In the following paragraphs, however, I want to attempt such an assess-

---

*Reprinted from the *Bucknell Review*, VII (No. 4, 1958), 234-240, by permission of the author and publisher. Copyright 1958 by the *Bucknell Review*.
[1]Cleanth Brooks, *Modern Poetry and the Tradition* (New York, 1939), pp. 226-227; Louis A. Landa, "*A Modest Proposal* and Populousness," *MP*, XL (Nov. 1942), 161-170, and George Wittkowsky, "Swift's *Modest Proposal*: The Biography of an Early Georgian Pamphlet," *JHI*, IV (Jan. 1943), 74-104; John M. Bullitt, "Ironic Masks," *Jonathan Swift and the Anatomy of Satire: A Study of Satiric Technique* (Cambridge, Mass., 1953), pp. 56-67, Martin Price, "The Ironic Mask," *Swift's Rhetorical Art: A Study in Structure and Meaning* (New Haven, 1953), pp. 57-74, and William Bragg Ewald, Jr., *The Masks of Jonathan Swift* (Oxford, 1954), pp. 163-175.

ment in the area of structure: to examine the effects won by Swift's arrangement of materials.

I need not inquire hypothetically what the essay would be like had it appeared in straightforward, conventional prose. Swift's sermon, "Causes of the Wretched Condition of Ireland," very/235/likely preached in the same period *A Modest Proposal* was published, deals with almost identical external subject matter and is similar in length (thirty paragraphs as compared with the *Proposal's* thirty-three).[2]

After an introductory paragraph, the sermon opens immediately with a statement of remedies in the power of the Irish to combat economic interference from England. The Irish, now only *"Hewers of Wood, and Drawers of Water"* for England, will approach freedom if they overcome their own vanity of buying foreign goods; if the Irish children are protected from habits of idleness and sloth; and if oppressing, often non-resident landlords are discouraged. The fourteen paragraphs devoted to the remedies are followed by eight on Swift's scheme for parish charity schools; six paragraphs on the deserving poor, who should be recognized as a parish responsibility and distinguished from professional beggars and strollers by the wearing of badges; and a paragraph of exhortation.

With its formal Biblical text ("That there be no complaining in our Streets. Happy is the People that is in such a Case") and tailpiece prayer ("The Grace of God, &c"), and with its plain, vigorous appeal to the reason of Swift's parishioners, who had learned to expect neither wit nor cant from him in the pulpit, the sermon is a very different species of discourse from *A Modest Proposal for preventing the Children of Poor People from being a Burthen to their Parents, or the Country, and for making them Beneficial to the Publick.* It could only by the greatest wrench of terminology be considered great literature, as the *Proposal* unquestionably is.

Yet if the first sentence of the sermon were exchanged for that of the essay, only persons expert in Swift's works would immediately guess it, for at first glance the constructions as well as the ideas seem hardly to differ:

It is a very melancholy Reflection, that such a Country as ours, which is capable of producing all Things nec-/236/essary and

---

[2] *"Causes of the Wretched Condition of Ireland* is extensive in scope, being a condensed statement of views that Swift treated more elaborately in the Irish tracts. . . . The sermon is a catalogue of complaints and indictments." See Louis A. Landa, "Introduction to the Sermons," in Jonathan Swift, *Irish Tracts, 1720-1723, And Sermons,* ed. Herbert Davis (Oxford, 1948), p. 128.

most Things convenient for Life, sufficient for the Support of four Times the Number of its Inhabitants, should yet lye under the heaviest Load of Misery and Want, our Streets crouded with Beggars, so many of our lower Sort of Tradesmen, Labourers and Artificers, not able to find Cloaths and Food for their Families.

* * * * *

It is a melancholly Object to those, who walk through this great Town, or travel in the Country, when they see the *Streets,* the *Roads,* and *Cabbin-Doors,* crowded with *Beggars* of the female Sex, followed by three, four, or six Children, *all in Rags,* and importuning every Passenger for an Alms.

The latter, from *A Modest Proposal,* is the more concise, concrete, and dramatic sentence. It severely limits itself, not to a "Reflection," but to the active impression of persons who "walk" or "travel" among the Irish beggars and "see" them "crowded," "followed," and "importuning"; and it modestly introduces the word "Children," to prepare for shocks to follow. Yet in isolation the sentence could not be thought remarkable: it becomes so only when it functions within the total structure of the essay. One characteristic aspect of the essay as a whole lies in the seeming prosaic innocence of the first sentence and of some following sentences that are meant to have the authentic sound of a sermon or tract.

Unlike his sermon Swift's essay wants time to reveal itself calculatedly — evoking a certain suspense, only partially disclosing the burden of its thought, producing the unexpected on several strata, and introducing seemingly irrelevant but artful flourishes of language — though its intention or desired end is precisely that of the sermon: to arouse the Irish and show ways to alleviate their wretched condition.

In the famous essay there are eight paragraphs introductory to the statement of the shocking, burlesque proposition that the fairest, cheapest method for helping Ireland is in breeding children to be sold for meat. Twenty paragraphs linger excruciatingly upon the "advantages" of such a plan. Then in a single paragraph, accompanied by a transitional sentence set off by itself, Swift's real propositions are proffered, the same serious proposals that form the bulk of the sermon, though here they are negatively phrased: "Therefore let no Man talk to me of other Expedients: *Of taxing/237/our Absentees at five Shillings a Pound: Of using neither Cloaths, nor household Furniture, except what is of our own Growth and Manufacture: ... Of curing the Expenciveness of Pride, Vanity, Idleness, and Gaming in our Women: Of introducing a Vein of Parcimony, Prudence and Temperance: ... Of teaching Landlords to have at least one Degree of Mercy towards their Tenants.*" There are ten such items, thick-coming and close-packed in their single paragraph, so obviously reasonable in contrast to the insanely logical elaborate plan for eating children that (if they can be read at all in the glare of the brilliant burlesque) they seem eminently workable. It is only in this crucial paragraph that the tension, created by assent to the *Proposal's* persuasive tone and rejection of its dreadful "matter," is resolved.[3]

Three paragraphs conclude the essay with the pretended speaker's turning attention upon himself and the kind of man he is ("But as to my self," "After all, I am not so violently bent upon my own opinion," and "I profess in the sincerity of my Heart"), almost in the same manner that the sermon ends with Swift in the role of pastor, turning with familiar phrases to consideration of his flock.

Much of the tension in *A Modest Proposal* lies in irony that is not at first apparent, contained within a design of seemingly/238/innocent phrases that have been artfully "planted" throughout the general structure of the essay. The patriotic or canting *"dear Native Country"* of the first paragraph is shown in its proper setting only after one turns back to it from the end of the essay, in which Ireland has been characterized as a place appalling to its poor, who would "think it a great Happiness to have been sold for Food." Yet before Swift's soberly intended proposals can be put into action, Ireland must become in reality a *"dear Native Country"* that its people have

---

[3] F. R. Leavis sees this tension as leading to indecision and exasperated frustration in the reader's mind. "The Irony of Swift," *Determinations* (London, 1934), pp. 79-108. Drawing upon Mr. Leavis's essay, Donald A. Davie calls the total effect of Swift's style in *A Modest Proposal* one of "painful indecision," leading nowhere: By comparison with Johnson and Berkeley, Swift seems sheerly irresponsible; and this is particularly true of Swift the ironist." "Irony and Conciseness in Berkeley and in Swift," *The Dublin Mag.*, XXVII (Oct.-Dec. 1952), 20-29. Both Mr. Leavis and Mr. Davie ignore the vital paragraph in which Swift states his serious proposals for action. John Middleton Murry takes the paragraph of serious remedies into consideration—but as the touchstone to defeat rather than as a call to action: "His efforts had ended in smoke. . . . So, in the *Modest Proposal*, he dismisses all the measures which he had specifically urged them [the Irish Protestants] to adopt. They had refused them; he now discards them, one by one." *Jonathan Swift: A Critical Biography* (London, 1954), p. 428.

The most recent reference to *A Modest Proposal* in this connection is that of Northrop Frye, who stresses the necessity of structural tension in all effective satire: "The argument of Swift's *Modest Proposal* has a brain-softening plausibility about it: one is almost led fo feel that the narrator is not only reasonable but even humane; yet the 'almost' can never drop out of any sane man's reaction, and as long as it remains there the modest proposal will be both fantastic and immoral. . . . Hence satire is irony which is structurally close to the comic: the comic struggle of two societies, one normal and the other absurd, is reflected in its double focus of morality and fantasy." *Anatomy of Criticism: Four Essays* (Princeton, 1957), p. 224.

learned to love. Similarly, before one learns precisely what the method is, the method for making children useful to the public seems perfectly acceptable in its initial description as "fair, cheap, and easy." Repeated in the penultimate paragraph these adjectives become despicable when the projector, having outlined his proposal, avows his willingness to listen an any other plan "equally Innocent, Cheap, Easy and Effectual." The real point — one of serious wit — is that the country cannot (the Irish must learn) be saved cheaply or easily.

As in poetry, a unifying intensity is achieved throughout the structure of the *Proposal* by means of a verbal contrivance that has been termed "the perpetual slight alteration of language." Words are juxtaposed in shifting combinations and in a variety of contexts: throughout the essay references to children vary from a context of seeming humanitarianism to a context of animality, and then to a context of vendible commodity, sometimes all three being expressed at once. The word "Children" appears in the title, and the final word in the piece is "Childbearing." At the outset one's sympathy is enlisted for "Children, *all in Rags*," "Children, in the Arms," "*helpless Infants*," "*poor innocent Babes*," and "Children of poor Parents." But as early as the fourth paragraph there is a clue to the animality to follow, in the reference to "a Child, *just dropt from its Dam*," though the unprepared reader would never guess that this leads to a recommendation for "buying the Children alive, and dressing them hot from the Knife, as we do *roasting Pigs*." After the proposal has been made, in the ninth paragraph, where "a young healthy Child" is equated with "a most delicious, nourishing, and wholesome Food," children are predominantly considered as a commodity: "this food," "Infant's flesh," "the *Carcass of a good fat Child*," a new Dish," "the Goods," "a well grown, fat Yearling Child," and "this kind of Commodity." After the proposal is almost complete,/239/in the twenty-sixth paragraph, the most offending allusion to children occurs — prepared for from the beginning — when, in a context of animality and commodity, one reads of "the poor Babes."

Swift's sermon on the "Causes of the Wretched Condition of Ireland" was intended to work directly upon its hearers, whereas *A Modest Proposal* is indirectly expressed through dramatic fiction, with Swift acting in character and addressing a fictional audience. Swift's relationship with his reader is indirect throughout; his relationship with his created *persona*, the projector, is almost — but not quite — antithetical.

Believing in the unquestionable authority of statistics, the self-deluded projector expects to inspire credence with his phrases of "I calculate," "I have reckoned," or "I have already computed." He is a "disinterested" businessman who accepts the economic materialism of his time as the sole grounds from which patriotic action ("good business") can conceivably begin. He insists upon practical expedients and prides himself upon his disinterestedness.

Swift himself was anything but disinterested. It cannot be said that in 1729 he devoted his entire energy to problems of Irish welfare, for he spent a few months on the estate of friends outside Dublin and considered building a house there; returned to Dublin to find his influence as the "Drapier" courted by both candidates in the elections; received "a gammon, the product of the wilds of America" from a Philadelphia Quaker; learned that some bottles of Irish usquebaugh intended for Lord Bolingbroke had not arrived in England; and said that now he mixed water with his wine, could eat only "half a dish of meat," still suffered from attacks of giddiness, and was reading ecclesiastical history. But he wrote with directness and passion to Alexander Pope, three months before the *Proposal* was advertised for sale (as an "excellent treatise"), that he was strongly agitated to see Ireland sunk in such dire circumstances:

> As to this country, there have been three terrible years' dearth of corn, and every place strewed with beggars; but dearths are common in better climates, and our evils here lie much deeper. Imagine a nation the two thirds of whose revenues are spent out of it, and who are not permitted to trade with the other third, and where the pride of women will not suffer them to wear their own/240/manufactures, even when they excel what come from abroad. This is the true state of Ireland in a very few words. These evils operate more every day, and the kingdom is absolutely undone, as I have been telling often in print these ten years past. What I have said requires forgiveness, but I had a mind for once to let you know the state of our affairs, and my reason for being more moved than perhaps becomes a clergyman, and a piece of a philosopher, and perhaps the increase of years and disorders may hope for some allowance to complaints especially when I may call myself a stranger in a strange land.[4]

Here in this highly affecting single paragraph the matter of the sermon and the famous essay appears in little — the seed from which the other two pieces, different as they are, grew.

---

[4] 11 Aug. 1729, *Corr.*, ed. F. E. Ball (London, 1910-14), IV, 89-90. (Pope could only reply: "I truly share in all that troubles you, and wish you removed from a scene of distress, which I know works your compassionate temper too strongly.")

In the *Proposal,* indirectly but unmistakably, through the trans-
lucid, chilling, mad logic of the projector, Swift can be heard speaking as clergyman and philosopher, his compassionate temper pas-
sionately moved. For the length of one sentence he merges with his
created speaker when he says: "But as to my self, having been
wearied out for many Years with offering vain, idle, visionary
thoughts, and at length utterly despairing of Success, I fortunately
fell upon this Proposal." This, I think, can be considered the voice
of Swift — as in his letter to Pope — speaking for himself, expressing his rejection of attempts to assist Ireland through his serious
pamphlets and sermons. Earlier in his life he had rejected his attempts to write serious odes ("There thy enchantment broke, and
from this hour,/ I here renounce thy visionary pow'r"). Just as he
had turned his interest and talent to the invention of witty satirical
verses, he now turns to the satirical structure of *A Modest Proposal.*[5]

---

[5] See my study, *The Sin of Wit: Jonathan Swift as a Poet* (Syracuse, 1950),
pp. 1-9; and "Swift's Renunciation of the Muse," *N&Q,* CXCVII (24 May 1952),
235-236.

Oliver W. Ferguson

Swift's *Saeva Indignatio* and *A Modest Proposal**

For two hundred years readers have admired Swift's *Modest Proposal* as one of the greatest pieces of sustained irony in the language. No one has failed to note the brilliance with which Swift balanced the opposing tones of the tract: the economic projector's studied disinterestedness and his own rage. But too little attention has been given to the object of that rage or to Swift's real purpose in the *Modest Proposal*.

The traditional assumption has been that it was upon England, and not Ireland, that he was venting his *saeva indignatio*. Leslie Stephen called the tract "the most complete expression of burning indignation against intolerable wrongs"; and Henry Craik concluded his brief discussion of it with a passionate rhetorical question: "Can England ever forget what lies on her conscience, while Swift's *Modest Proposal* continues to be read?" This position has for the most part been adopted by later critics. W. A. Eddy cites Walpole, Wood, and absentee English landlords as the immediate objects of Swift's attack and sees that attack as Swift's outraged protest against the brutality of England's exploitation of Ireland. Ricardo Quintana, both in *The Mind and Art of Jonathan Swift* and the recent *Swift, An Introduction*, gives only the most general account of the tract, noting its irony and Swift's consummate use of the rhetorical device termed by Pons *le mythe animal*. A much more important study, Louis Landa's "*A Modest Proposal* and Populousness," shows Swift's use of mercantilist theory in the tract, but argues that in terms of this theory Swift's

---

*Reprinted from *Philological Quarterly*, XXXVIII (October, 1959), 473-479, by permission of the author and the publisher. Copyright 1959 by the University of Iowa.

satire was doubly damaging to *England* because her misrule in Ireland had there invalidated universal economic laws, especially the
fundamental mercantilist maxim that people are the riches of a nation. George Wittkowsky, in his "Swift's *Modest Proposal:* the
Biography of an Early Georgian Pamphlet," is also interested in the
part contemporary economic theory played in Swift's tract, and he
reads the *Modest Proposal* as chiefly a parody on current expressions
of this theory. Similar to this view is that of Herbert Davis, who, in
The Satire of Jonathan Swift, says that Swift's irony is directed
against serious/474/proposals which "take no account of the determined policy of the English government to impoverish the Irish
people."[1]

It is the purpose of the present study to show that Swift's anger in
the *Modest Proposal* was directed towards Ireland, not England, and
that the tract was his carefully itemized indictment of every class of
Irish life, down to and including the very beggars. Further, it will
show that Swift's view of the Irish was that of the defeated moral
reformer, and it will show how this view determines the mode and
tone of Swift's satire in the tract. It should be made clear that such
a reading does not deny England's role in Ireland's tragedy or Swift's
awareness of that role (there is, of course, a reference to England in
the tract); rather, it emphasizes Swift's primary aim in writing the
last major piece he ever published on Irish affairs.

A Modest Proposal was written, the projector tells us, because he
had "been wearied out for many Years with offering vain, idle,
visionary Thoughts."[2] These "Thoughts" were Swift's own tracts
written from 1720 to 1729, tracts which had touched on practically
every aspect of Ireland's economy and which were directed solely to

---

[1] Leslie Stephen, *Swift* (London, 1889), p. 165; Henry Craik, *The Life of
Jonathan Swift* (London, 1894), II, 155; W. A. Eddy, *Swift's Satires and Personal
Writings* (London & New York, 1932), p. 20; Ricardo Quintana, *The Mind and
Art of Jonathan Swift* (London, 1953), p. 346; Quintana, *Swift, An Introduction*
(London & New York, 1955), pp. 176-77; Louis Landa, *"A Modest Proposal* and
Populousness," *Modern Philology,* XL (1942-43), 162; George Wittkowsky,
"Swift's *Modest Proposal:* the Biography of an Early Georgian Pamphlet," *Jour-
nal of the History of Ideas,* IV (1943), 74-104; Herbert Davis, *The Satire of Jonathan
Swift* (New York, 1947), p. 107. In his Introduction to Vol. XII of Swift's *Prose
Works* (Oxford, 1955), Dr. Davis modifies his earlier view to the extent of saying
that the *Modest Proposal* was addressed to an Irish audience (p. xx). John
Middleton Murry, in his *Jonathan Swift* (London, 1954), reads Swift's satire in
too narrow a scope in seeing the Protestant ruling class in Ireland as the object
of Swift's attack in the *Modest Proposal* (p. 429).

[2] *The Prose Works of Jonathan Swift,* ed. Herbert Davis (Oxford, 1955), XII,
117. All subsequent quotations from *A Modest Proposal* are taken from this
edition.

the Irish. In them Swift had considered the projects of other men and had advanced his own in a constant effort to stir Ireland from her lethargy — projects to establish a local mint, to introduce farm and road improvements, to encourage fair dealing among shopkeepers and tenants, and to discourage the excessive emigration that was depopulating the country. In fact, this newest proposal of 1729 was but a logical extension of a plea Swift had made unceasingly to the people of Ireland: domestic consumption of domestic products. It is in outlining the advantages of this latest plan that/475/Swift systematically condemns the landlords, the idle rich of both sexes, the Irish poor, Protestant Dissenters, Papists, absentees, shopkeepers—in short, "the whole people of Ireland."

The commodity, the projector admits, will be "somewhat dear, and therefore very *proper for Landlords;* who, as they have already devoured most of the Parents, seem to have the best Title to the Children" (p. 112). This, it should be noted, is a reference to *Irish* landlords, whether resident or absentee; as early as 1720, Swift was castigating "our Country Landlords" for their selfish unconcern with the welfare of Ireland.[3] Continuing his attack on the upper classes, the projector notes that the scheme will appeal to "all *Gentlemen of Fortune* in the Kingdom, who have any refinement in Taste" — whose lavish manner of living Swift had sought to curb through sumptuary laws. For such epicures, a clever cook will be able to make the new delicacy "as expensive as they please" (p. 115). And the "Gentlemen of Fortune" were not alone in their extravagance. At one point the projector directs a vicious aside to the women of fashion — whose ruinous demands for imported luxuries Swift had assailed for years: Though he rejects the "Refinement" of his scheme offered by a friend, that the eligible age limit of the children be extended to fourteen, he confesses that the kingdom would benefit if it could thus destroy "several plump young girls in this Town, who . . . appear at the *Playhouse,* and *Assemblies* in foreign Fineries, which they never will pay for" (p. 114).

The lowest class of native Irish do not escape Swift's wrath: In addition to being economically advantageous, the scheme will teach the Irish poor common humaneness (the severity of the irony here attests to Swift's disgust at the brutish ways of the "mere Irish"). During his wife's pregnancy, a man will curb his usual brutality for fear of causing a miscarriage (p. 115), and the new economic value

---

[3] *Prose Works,* ed. Davis, IX, 21.

of children will decrease the number of abortions and infanticides —
crimes which the projector says are committed "more to avoid the
Expense than the Shame" (p. 110). Further, in his unwittingly callous way the projector will allow one male for every four females,
because "these Children are seldom the Fruits of Marriage, *a Circumstance not much regarded by our Savages*" (p. 111). This charge
(a strange one to make against Catholic Ireland!) is Swift's con-
temptuous reference to the marriages performed among the Irish
poor by "couple-beggars," Roman priests who officiated at /476/
clandestine and—certainly from an Anglican point of view—illegal
ceremonies.[4]

Swift even found an occasion to aim a gibe at his old enemies the
Dissenters. Like many other writers on Irish affairs, he was alarmed
at the widespread emigration, especially by Ulster Presbyterians,
that was depleting the country of its people; and he angrily rejected
the Dissenters' claim that they were leaving Ireland because of Anglican oppression. The projector's scheme will decrease the number of
Catholics and thus partially restore the balance which was in danger
of being upset by so many "*good Protestants*" emigrating rather than
paying tithes "against their Conscience, to an idolatrous *Episcopal
Curate*" (p. 114).

These complaints, however, are incidental to the final, cumulative
indictment of the nation. Losing for a moment his willingness to
yield to a better patriot, the projector exclaims, "Let no man talk to
me of other Expedients," and he then lists such "expedients." The
important thing to note here is not that these had been proposed by
Swift since 1720 — almost every compiler of an anthology in which
the tract is reprinted has made this obvious point — but that they
had been proposed to the people of Ireland. Not one even remotely
applies to England; Swift does not here mention legislative or commercial restrictions. Like the proposal at hand, the rejected expedients had been in Ireland's own power to effect: to tax absentees; to
use products of native growth and manufacture; to refrain from
importing luxuries; to imbue all the people with a sense of morality,
cooperation, and patriotism (pp. 116-117).

"The two principal Branches of Preaching," Swift wrote in 1720,
"are first to tell the People what is their Duty; and then to convince
them that it is so."[5] From the *Proposal for the Universal Use of Irish
Manufacture* (1720) to the economic treatises of 1728-29, Swift had

---

[4] See W. E. H. Lecky, *A History of Ireland in the Eighteenth Century* (London,
1892), I, 382.
[5] *Prose Works*, ed. Davis, IX, 70.

been "preaching" to the people of Ireland, trying to convince them of their duty. It was, as he saw it, to improve to whatever degree possible Ireland's tottering economy. In a sermon on the causes of the country's condition, he acknowledged that Ireland suffered from many disadvantages "not by our own Faults," but in the same sermon he urged the people to try "what Remedies are in our Power towards removing, at least, some Part of these Evils."[6] With the exception of their resistance to Wood's Halfpence,/477/however, the Irish had failed in their duty. Instead of listening to the advice of men who were trying to help them, or following the simple dictates of common sense, the people persisted in the practices which, along with English oppression, contributed to their ruin. And as Ireland's "beggars" included "all *Cottagers, Labourers,* and Four fifths of the *Farmers*" (p. 112), so Ireland's guilt was shared by all Irishmen: the gentry, the tradesmen, the farmers — even, in some measure, the beggars. The gentry continued to import luxuries and to neglect agriculture. The shopkeepers and common laborers continued in their knavish and sottish ways. And at the very bottom of the social scale, the beggars — more sinning than sinned against — continued to infest the country, their idleness and wretchedness representing in small the state of the whole nation: "As a great part of our publick miseries is originally owing to our own faults," Swift wrote in 1737, "so I am confident, that among the meaner people, nineteen in twenty of those who are reduced to a starving condition, did not become so by what lawyers call the work of God ... but merely from their own idleness, attended with all manner of vices, particularly drunkenness, thievery, and cheating."[7]

That Swift adopted the technique of the political arithmeticians in *A Modest Proposal* should not obscure his intent. He was not concerned with satirizing the proposals of other writers on Irish affairs — men like Viscount Molesworth, Thomas Prior, Alexander Macaulay, Arthur Dobbs, James McCulla, and Sir John Browne. Far from disagreeing with them, Swift shared many of their economic theories. He mentioned with approval the work of Molesworth and Prior, and he openly sponsored Macaulay's *Some Thoughts on the Tillage of Ireland* with a prefatory letter of commendation. Nowhere in his works is there a reference to Dobbs, but he must have approved of an author who reflected so many of his own beliefs. With Browne and McCulla he was not in agreement, but in his answers to them he ob-

---

6 *Prose Works,* ed. Davis, IX, 199.
7 *The Prose Works of Jonathan Swift,* ed. Temple Scott (London, 1925), VII, 330.

jected to particular proposals and not to the authors as "projectors"; and he respected their intentions.[8] Whatever parody Swift employed in the *Modest Proposal* at the expense of such writers was to show their foolishness — like his own — in trying to help an indifferent Ireland.

When Swift's real purpose is understood, the use of *le mythe animal* in the *Modest Proposal* is seen to be more than an effective/478/ and convenient device. It is a point of view integral to Swift's judgment of Ireland. Swift is saying to the Irish, in effect, "You have acted like beasts; hence you no longer deserve the title of men."[9] A passage from a tract written some seven months before *A Modest Proposal* anticipates this point of view. Swift wondered, he wrote,

> whether those animals which come in my way with two legs and human faces, clad, and erect, be of the same species with what I have seen very like them in England, as to the outward Shape, but differing in their notions, natures, and intellectualls more than any two kinds of Brutes in a forest, which any men of common prudence would immediately discover, by persuading them to define what they mean by Law, Liberty, Property, Courage, Reason, Loyalty, or Religion.[10]

These animals the preacher had tried to show their duty; but their sloth and viciousness had defeated him. "I am banished," he wrote a friend in 1732, "to a country of slaves and beggars — my blood soured, my spirits sunk, fighting with beasts like St. Paul, not at Ephesus, but in Ireland."[11]

Further, it is *le mythe animal* that allows Swift to make the one proposal so singularly appropriate to this abandoned nation—cannibalism. It is the Irish, not the English, who are to commit the final

---

[8] *Prose Works*, ed. Davis, IX, 58-59; *The Drapier's Letters*, ed. Davis (Oxford, 1935), pp. 157 & 317; *Prose Works*, ed. Davis, XII, 22 & 97.

[9] It is just possible that the motif actually comes from the Americas, as the projector tells us (p. 111). In the *Commentarios Reales*, by Garcilaso de la Vega (1609-1617 [?]; English translation, 1688), is an account of how the Peruvians ate their own children. Whether Swift knew Garcilaso is impossible to say. However, it is interesting to know that Bolingbroke probably did. In *Reflections Concerning Innate Moral Principles*, attributed to Bolingbroke, there is a reference to Garcilaso's "Man-Eaters" with the comment, "We should never find whole Nations butchering their Kindred, and their Offspring, as we never find whole Nations destroying themselves" (London: S. Bladon, 1752, p. 63). It was just because Swift found such a thing in Ireland that he wrote *A Modest Proposal*.

[10] *Prose Works*, ed. Davis, XII, 65.

[11] *The Correspondence of Jonathan Swift*, ed. F. E. Ball (London, 1910-14), IV, 357.

barbarity, the last indignity to human reason, of eating their children. And the paradox of their position accounts for the ambivalence
between pity and wrath that Swift shows in the *Modest Proposal*.
The wretchedness which surrounds him *is* a "melancholly Object"
to Swift—the strolling mothers with their children, the young laborers unable to find work, the aged dying "as fast as can reasonably be
expected." But the more melancholy the object, the greater Swift's
anger at the object itself; for he saw the Irish as at once victims and
villains, by their criminal folly and selfishness devouring themselves.

If Ireland rather than England is the object of Swift's attack in the
Modest Proposal, it follows that Swift is not so far removed/479/
from the ingenuous "projector" as has been supposed.[12] For the projector's remedy for the Irish is a hyperbolic parallel to Swift's aban-
donment of them. In their conception of the Irish as beasts, Swift
and the projector are one. The crucial difference is in their attitudes
towards this conception: The projector's is economic; Swift's is
moral.[13] It is a mistake to speak of Swift interrupting in his own
voice in the key "other Expedients" passage. The voice is the same,
and the weary impatience with which these expedients are rejected
as "visionary Thoughts" is the same. Similarly, the reference to England at the conclusion of the tract (p. 117) is inconsistent not because Swift drowns out the projector's voice with his own, but
because he momentarily diverts the direction of his attack.[14]

In *A Modest Proposal*, ten years of warning and exhortation gave
way to frustration and despair, and Swift directed the full weight of
his anger not against England, or callous economists, or visionary
projectors, but against Ireland herself. Savage as this expression of
his anger is, a tract written in 1728 contains a passage even more
terrible than any in the *Modest Proposal*:

> If so wretched a State of Things would allow it, methinks I
> could have a malicious Pleasure, after all the Warning I have in
> vain given the Publick . . . to see the Consequences and Events
> answering in every Particular. I pretend to no Sagacity: What I

---

[12] See, for example, Ricardo Quintana, "Situational Satire: A Commentary on
the Method of Swift," *University of Toronto Quarterly*, XVII (1947-48), 130.

[13] The technique is similar to that in the *Argument against Abolishing Christianity*, where both Swift and the defender of nominal Christianity accept the
necessity of the Established Church, but do so for different reasons.

[14] For an example of the view that in these passages the projector is out of character, see W. B. Ewald, *The Masks of Jonathan Swift* (Cambridge, Mass., 1954),
pp. 171 & 173.

writ was little more than what I had discoursed to several Persons, who were generally of my Opinion: And it was obvious to every common Understanding, that such Effects must needs follow from such Causes . . . . *Wisdom crieth in the Streets; because I have called and ye refused; I have stretched out my Hand, and no Man regarded. But ye have set at nought all my Counsel, and would none of my Reproof. I also will laugh at your Calamity, and mock when your Fear cometh.*[15]

Here, stripped of all irony and grounded in the authority of Scripture, is the moralist's judgment on the people of Ireland.

---

[15] *Prose Works*, ed. Davis, XII, 22-23.

Edward P. J. Corbett

A Method of Analyzing Prose Style with a Demonstration Analysis of Swift's "A Modest Proposal"*

Most of us teachers have felt rather frustrated in our efforts to analyze prose style, either for ourselves or for our students in the classroom. This frustration has been brought on not only by a certain vagueness about what style is but also by the lack of a technique for analyzing prose style. As a result, we content ourselves in the classroom with enunciating such general, subjective labels for a particular author's style as "vigorous," "urbane," "ponderous," "curt," "mannered," "jaunty," "explosive," and that favorite all-purpose epithet "smooth-flowing." Some of us may have arrived at the point where we feel confident enough to designate more specific features of a prose style, such as the preponderance of Latinate diction, the mannerism of balanced sentence structure, or the high proportion of concrete images. But usually by the time we have gone that far, we have exhausted our resources for describing prose style, and we spend the rest of the class period discussing the ideas of the essay under consideration.

The New Criticism, especially as it was presented in Brooks and Warren's influential textbook *Understanding Poetry*, gave us teachers a technique for analyzing the verbal strategies of a poem. Consequently, we feel very secure when we come to analyze poetry for or with our students. What we need now is comparable training in a method of analyzing prose style.

What would lay the groundwork for the development of such a method would be a number of descriptions of prose style comparable

---

*Reprinted from *Reflections on High School English*, edited by Gary Tate (Tulsa: The University of Tulsa, 1966), pp. 106-124, by permission of the author, the editor, and the publisher. Copyright 1966 by the University of Tulsa.

to the descriptions of English grammar that we have had from modern linguists. It is surprising how few of these studies have been produced. At the end of the last century, Edwin H. Lewis's *The History of the English Paragraph* (University of Chicago Studies, 1894), L. A. Sherman's *Some Observations upon Sentence-Length/107/ in English Prose* (University of Nebraska Studies, 1892), and G. W. Gerwig's *On the Decrease of Predication and of Sentence Weight in English* (University of Nebraska Studies, 1894) presented statistical studies of several prose stylists. In this century, we have had a few stylistic studies of specific authors, such as Warner Taylor's *The Prose Style of Johnson* (Madison, 1918), Zilpha E. Chandler's *An Analysis of the Stylistic Techniques of Addison, Johnson, Hazlitt and Pater* (Iowa City, 1928), and W. K. Wimsatt's *The Prose Style of Samuel Johnson* (New Haven, 1941).[1] Very shortly, I understand, Mouton of the Hague will publish Louis Milic's study of Jonathan Swift's style.

As more of these stylistic descriptions appear, we will gain a basis for more valid generalizations about English prose style, and we may find that we have to relinquish some of our illusions about how certain writers create their stylistic effects. Such studies will also help us to develop techniques for analyzing style and to prepare textbooks for the classroom. Those of us who are interested in doing something with style in the classroom are looking forward to the publication of textbooks on style now being prepared by such teachers as Richard Ohmann, Francis Christensen, Winston Weathers and Otis Winchester, Harriet Sheridan, and Josephine Miles.

I will outline here a procedure for analyzing prose style. There will be very little in this proposed method that is original. I have merely brought together what I have learned about style from the ancient rhetoricians and from modern expositors of verbal strategies. After I have outlined the various features of style that one might look for in studying any prose piece, I will illustrate the method with a fairly detailed analysis of one of the most anthologized prose essays in English literature, Jonathan Swift's *A Modest Proposal*.

Any stylistic analysis must start out, I think, with some close observation of what actually appears on the printed page. One might, for instance, sense that a particular author uses a great many short sentences. Now, sentence-length is one of the features that can tell

---

[1] We must not forget, of course, the pioneering work that Morris W. Croll did in the 1920's on sixteenth and seventeenth-century English prose style. These studies will soon be published in a single volume.

us something about an author's style. But it should be obvious that we cannot make a tenable generalization about an author's characteristic sentence-length until we have determined, by some rather tedious counting and tabulating, just how long or short his sentences are. Such a procedure would make counters and measures of us all— "a slide-rule method," to use Leslie Whipp's term,[2] that we humanistically trained teachers may find repellent—but this is a necessary step if we are to learn something about style in general and about style in particular.

If teachers and students survive the tedium of such counting/108/ and tabulating, they will then have a chance to bring to bear their aesthetic sensibilities. The next step in the procedure — and a more significant step—is to relate what the statistics reveal to the rhetoric of the piece being analyzed. Determining the length of a prose sentence is much like scanning a line of verse. Just as it is fairly easy to determine that a particular line of verse is written in iambic pentameter, so it is easy to determine that a particular sentence in prose is, say, twenty-one words long. But so what? The more important consideration is the function of that meter or that sentence-length. What contribution does this meter or this sentence-length make to the effect that the writer was seeking to produce? Here is where our judgment or our aesthetic sensibility or our rhetorical sense will have an opportunity to exercise itself. And it is here, in our relating of fact to function, that we will experience a perceptible growth in our powers of analysis and criticism.

A note of caution should be raised at this point. Inductive logic has taught us that the strength of a generalization rests partly on the number of observed facts. Just as one swallow does not make a summer so a prevalent stylistic feature observed in a single piece of prose does not necessarily constitute a characteristic of the author's style. An author's style may change as his subject-matter or his purpose or his audience changes. Moreover, his style may have evolved over a period of time, and the stylistic feature that we have observed in this particular prose piece may be a mannerism that he eventually outgrew. True, certain characteristics of an author's style will be fairly constant, but we would be wise to withhold any generalizations about those constants until after we have studied a reasonably large body of a man's prose. All that we may be able to conclude from our inductive study of a single essay is that this

---

[2] See Leslie T. Whipp and Margaret E. Ashida, "A Slide-Rule Composition Course," *College English*, XXV (October, 1963), 18-22.

particular stylistic device is a feature of this particular prose piece. But of course even that limited generalization represents some gain in our knowledge of an author's style.

Another caution is that we must be careful in our effort to relate fact to function. Dr. Johnson, you recall, said about Pope's celebrated doctrine of suiting sound to the sense, "This notion of representative metre, and the desire of discovering frequent adaptations of the sound to the sense, have produced, in my opinion, many wild conceits and imaginary beauties." We can indeed become excessively ingenious in our efforts to make a stylistic feature fit a rhetorical function. The pitfalls of such speculation, however, should not discourage us from at least making the attempt. Even a strained speculation about the aptness of a particular stylistic feature is better than leaving an observed fact hanging in mid-air./109/We can later revise or reject our forced speculation when our knowledge or skill grows. If I may indulge in a platitude, nothing ventured, nothing gained.

With these general observations and cautions about the method in mind, we can now look at a listing of some of the objectively observable features of style. These features will be considered under the three main heads of words, sentences, and paragraphs.

What is there that we can observe about words or, to use the more common rhetorical term, diction? Well, we can seek to determine whether an author's diction is predominantly general or specific; abstract or concrete; formal or informal; polysyllabic or monosyllabic; common or special; referential or emotive. Judgments about the either-or will be more subjective in some cases than in others. We can, for instance, determine precisely the proportion between monosyllabic and polysyllabic diction; but since the difference between, say, formal and informal diction is relative, our judgments about some words on this score will necessarily be subjective. Making allowances for those subjective judgments, however, we still can determine, in cases of relative difference, the general tenor of a man's diction. After studying the diction of an A. J. Liebling piece on boxing, for instance, we would find it fairly easy to conclude that although Mr. Liebling adroitly mixes formal and informal words, his diction is predominantly informal.

The frequency of proper nouns in a piece will also tell us something about a man's style. In the readability formula that Rudolf Flesch devised several years ago, the incidence of proper nouns was one of the factors that enhanced the readability of prose. Then too there will always be some few words in an essay that will tell us a great deal about an author's period, milieu, range of interest, education, and bias. We would do well to look for such indicative words.

Studying the diction of a prose piece from these various angles will help us to determine the "weight" of a man's style and to account for the effect that a man's style creates. Sometimes, for instance, when we get the general impression that a man's style is heavy and opaque, we are surprised to learn, after a close study of the diction, that the peculiar texture of his style has *not* been produced by his choice of words. And that kind of revelation is a real gain for us, because then we know that we will have to look elsewhere for the cause of the ponderous effect.

In moving on from a study of word-choice to a study of words in collocation, we find that the most fruitful syntactical unit to study is the sentence. What can we look for when we study the sentences in a prose piece? For one thing, we can study the length of sentences (measured in number of words). Once the total number of /110/ sentences and the total number of words are known, we can, by a simple exercise in long division, figure out the average sentence-length. We can then get an idea of variations of sentence-length by tabulating the percentage of sentences which *exceed,* and the percentage which *fall short of,* the average by a specified number of words.

One can also make a study of the *kinds* of sentences in a prose piece. One can tabulate the grammatical types of sentences (simple, compound, complex, compound-complex); or the rhetorical types (loose, periodic, balanced, antithetical); or the functional types (statement, question, command, exclamation). In studying varieties of sentence patterns, one can look at such things as inversions of normal word-order, the frequency and kinds of sentence-openers (infinitive, gerund, or participial phrases; adverb clauses; absolute constructions; expletive patterns; conjunctive words and phrases); and the methods and location of expansion in the sentences.

Although tropes (words with transferred meanings) could be observed when we are studying diction, and schemes (unusual sentence patterns) could be observed when we are studying sentences, it is probably better to make a separate step of recording figures of speech. Under tropes we would be noting such things as metaphor, simile, synecdoche, metonymy, irony, litotes, oxymoron, antonomasia. Under schemes we would be noting such things as anaphora, apposition, parallelism, antithesis, chiasmus, climax, anastrophe. The study of schemes and tropes can reveal a great deal about the degree of vividness, vivacity, and ornateness in an author's style.

The rhetoric of the next largest unit, the paragraph, has been one of the most neglected aspects of stylistic study. Modern rhetoric books have paid a great deal of attention to the topic sentence, to the various methods of developing paragraphs, and to the qualities of unity, coherence, and emphasis, but a study of these aspects does not reveal very much about a man's style. Perhaps the reason why classical rhetorics did not deal at all with the paragraph is that classical rhetoric was concerned primarily with spoken discourse. Paragraphing of course is a typographical device to punctuate units of thought in written discourse only, and this kind of punctuation often reveals no more about a man's style than the punctuation used within sentences. But there must be an approach to the study of the paragraph that would reveal something about style, and perhaps Professor Francis Christensen's projected book on the rhetoric of the sentence and paragraph will provide the approach that will yield significant information about the style of the paragraph.

As a beginning, meanwhile, we can look at such things as the length of paragraphs (measured in number of words and/or number/111/ of sentences), the various levels of movement or development in the paragraph, the means of articulating sentences within the paragraph, and the transitional devices used between paragraphs. By observing the length of paragraphs and the modes of development and articulation, we will get a sense of the density, pace, and readability of an author's style.

The tabulation of objectively observable items, such as I have been outlining, might be called the stage of "gathering the data." It is a wearisome, time-consuming inductive exercise, but it is a necessary stage if our generalizations about a man's style are to be at all tenable. Needless to say, one does not have to look at *all* of the features in every stylistic analysis, and one does not have to follow the order outlined above. Sometimes concentration on a few salient features will bring us closer to the essence of a man's style than will an exhaustive analysis. Style is a complex of many linguistic devices cooperating to produce a peculiar effect, but it may not always be necessary to expose all of the linguistic devices in order to account for the effect.

Let me recommend one fruitful practice for this gathering of the data. You might try copying out by hand long passages of the essay or even the entire essay. You will be amazed at the number of additional things you will detect about a man's style when you write out his text. From my experience with transcribing a text, I would estimate that by copying you will detect at least three times as many features as you will by merely reading and rereading the text. In gathering the data for my analysis of Swift's *A Modest Proposal*, I detected some of the most significant features of his style only after I had laboriously copied out the entire text of the essay.

Gathering the data is a prelude for the more important, the more difficult stage—relating this data to the author's rhetorical strategies. It does not take much intelligence to gather the data; it takes only patience and accuracy. But it does take intelligence and perhaps a good measure of imagination to be able to see the rhetorical function of a particular stylistic feature.

The "why" of any stylistic feature can be answered only in relation to something else — the subject-matter or the occasion or the genre or the author's purpose or the nature of the audience or the ethos of the writer. To be able to relate stylistic features to their rhetorical function then, we must have a secure knowledge of the essay we are analyzing. As a minimum, we must know its purpose, its thesis, and its organization. In addition, we may need to know something about the author, something about the situation that prompted the essay, something about the audience to whom the essay was directed. We should be able to gain a good/112/deal of this kind of knowledge from internal evidence alone. But we may find it helpful to resort to external sources in order to supplement what internal evidence tells us. So we may have to turn to biographical reference works, to literary histories, to critical articles. The point is that the more profound our understanding of the essay is, the easier it will be to relate a stylistic feature to its rhetorical function.

Before launching into my analysis of *A Modest Proposal*, let me suggest some follow-up exercises. Once your students have done an analysis of one or more stylistic features of an essay, they can be asked to study another essay by the same author. They may discover thereby that an author's style changes noticeably as his subject-matter or his purpose or his audience changes. The value to your students of such an observation will be the realization that an author must be in command, not of one style but of many styles. Next, you may want to direct your students to study another author, either from the same period or from a later period, preferably an author writing on a similar subject or with a similar purpose. Such comparisons can make meaningful to the students Buffon's famous statement, "Style is the man." And such comparisons can also make the students aware that styles change not only as the subject or genre or audience or purpose changes but as the period changes. Twentieth-century style in general is distinctively different from seventeenth-century style, and it will represent a real gain in the students' education if they come to realize that the radical changes in modern man's way of life have had a marked influence on the dominant style of the age.

Eventually, students should be turned loose on an analysis of their own prose style. This exercise may well be the most fruitful one for the students. They will be fascinated not only by what they learn about their own style but also by what they learn from comparing their style with that of professional writers. Let us hope that the students will be intelligent enough to recognize that the differences between their style and other authors' styles do not mean that their style is necessarily inferior to the styles of the other authors.

The best themes I have received from students during my teaching career have been those written by freshmen who were asked to comment on what they had learned from a series of stylistic studies. One of the reasons why these themes were fascinating enough to keep me up until 2:00 in the morning reading them was, I think, that the students were writing from a body of specific knowledge that they themselves had derived inductively. In other words, the problem of invention having been solved for them, the students had something to say—and somehow, for the first time,/113/they were finding apt words to say what they had to say. Try this with your students. You may for the first time in your teaching career become excited about a batch of themes.

I have gone on long enough now about a general procedure for analyzing prose style. The method should become more meaningful for you as I apply it to a specific piece of prose—in this case, Jonathan Swift's famous satirical essay *A Modest Proposal*.

I might begin this stylistic analysis by defining what kind of discourse *A Modest Proposal* is, since genre makes its own demands on the kind of style that an author will employ. With reference to the literary genres, *A Modest Proposal* can be classified as a satire, and with reference to the four forms of discourse, satire must be classified as argumentation. If we were using the classical rhetorician's three kinds of persuasive discourse to further specify what type of argumentation we have here, we would classify *A Modest Proposal* as an instance of "deliberative" discourse, since Jonathan Swift is bent on changing the attitude of the propertied class toward the Irish poor and ultimately on moving this class to take some action that would remedy the lot of the poor.

In 1728, a year before *A Modest Proposal* was published, there had been a devastating famine in Ireland caused by three successive failures of the harvest. This famine had aggravated the misery of a people that had already been reduced to abject poverty by years of heavy taxation, repressive laws, and absentee landlordism. As Louis A. Landa has pointed out,[3] Swift hoped to expose the contradiction between a favorite maxim of the mercantilist economic writers— namely, that people are the riches of a nation — and the practice of reducing the majority of subjects to a condition of grinding poverty. The prevalence of the poverty was plain to see, and there had been no lack of proposals, from the political economists, of ways to remedy the condition of the poor. But the ruling class and the absentee land- lords were not listening; battening on the revenues from the land, they were not much concerned about the condition of the peasants who were producing their wealth. Swift was determined to get their ear. He would shock them into attention. And he would shock them into attention with a monstrous proposal presented by means of two of his favorite satiric techniques—using a mask and using irony.

To make his use of the mask or *persona* effective, Swift must create a character who is consistent, credible, and authoritative. This must be a character who, in a sense, "sneaks up" on the reader, a character who lulls the reader into expecting a sensible, practicable solution of the Irish problem and who, even after he has dropped his bomb- shell, maintains his pose and his poise. This character will exert a curious kind of ethical appeal—a man who/114/at the beginning of the essay gives the impression of being serious, expert, and well- meaning but who gradually reveals himself to be shockingly inhuman and naive. The character that eventually emerges is that of a fool whose insanity becomes, as Martin Price puts it, "a metaphor for the guilt of responsible men."[4]

One of the consequences of this use of a *persona* is that the style of the essay will not be Swift's style; rather it will be a style appro- priate to the character that Swift has created. True, some of the characteristics of Swift's style will be present; no author can entirely submerge his own style, except perhaps when he is engaged in writ- ing a parody of another author's style. But if Swift does his job properly, the message of the essay will be conveyed to us in a style that differs, at least in some respect, from the style that Swift displays when he is speaking in his own voice.

One of the respects in which the style of *A Modest Proposal* differs noticeably from Swift's usual style is the sentence-length. The aver- age sentence-length in this essay is 56.9 words per sentence. And we

[3] See Louis A. Landa, "*A Modest Proposal* and Populousness," *Modern Phil- ology*, XL (1942), 161-170 and "Swift's Economic Views and Mercantilism," *Jour- nal of Literary History*, X (1942), 310-335.

[4] Martin Price, *Swift's Rhetorical Art* (New Haven: Yale University Press, 1953), p. 88.

note some remarkable variations above and below that average. Although 46% of his sentences are composed of less than 47 words, almost 30% of his sentences are longer than 67 words (see Appendix for additional statistics on sentence-length). It is interesting to compare this sentence-length with that in two other works where Swift used a *persona*. In studying 200 paragraphs of *Gulliver's Travels* and 100 paragraphs of *A Tale of a Tub*, Edwin Herbert Lewis discovered the average sentence-length to be 40.7 words—almost 50% shorter than the average sentence in *A Modest Proposal*.[5] What has happened to the "conciseness" that Herbert Davis says is the most distinctive quality of Swift's style?[6] What has happened of course is that in *A Modest Proposal* we are listening to a man who is so filled with his subject, so careful about qualifying his statements and computations, so infatuated with the sound of his own words, that he rambles on at inordinate length.

We note this same tendency to qualify and ramify his thoughts in other characteristics of the proposer's sentence structure. We note this, for one thing, in his frequent use of parentheses. Sometimes the parenthetical matter throws in a gratuitous aside—"(as I must confess the times require)"; or editorializes—"(although indeed very unjustly)"; or qualifies a statement—"(I mean in the country)"; or insinuates an abrupt note of ethical appeal—"(it would, I think with humble submission, be a loss to the public)." Interpolated gestures like these, especially when they are as frequent as they are in this essay, betray a man who is unusually concerned for the accuracy of his statements and for the image he is projecting to his audience.

Something of the same tendency is evident in the many absolute /115/constructions in the essay. Most of these occur at the end of fairly long sentences—e.g. "the charge of nutriment and rags having been at least four times that value" (para. 7); "their corn and cattle being seized and money a thing unknown" (para. 33). These trailing-off phrases create the effect of a thought suddenly remembered and desperately thrown in. What is clever, though, about Swift's use of these trailing-off phrases, placed as they are in an emphatic position, is that in many cases they carry the real sting of the sentence. Here is that topsy-turviness of values that constitutes one of the main strate-

---

[5] Edwin H. Lewis, *History of the English Paragraph* (Chicago: University of Chicago Press, 1894), pp. 35-36.

[6] Herbert Davis, "The Consciseness of Swift," *Essays on the Eighteenth Century Presented to David Nichol Smith* (Oxford: at the Clarendon Press, 1945), pp. 15-32.

gies of the essay—important things couched in ironical terms or hidden away in weak structures.

This tendency to ramify, qualify, or refine statements is evident too in the proposer's habit of compounding elements. I am referring not so much to the common eighteenth-century practice of using doublets and triplets, of which there are a conspicuous number in *A Modest Proposal*, as to the proposer's habit of stringing out words and phrases beyond the common triad, so that we get the effect almost of an exhaustive cataloguing of details or qualifiers. I am referring to instances like these:

> stewed, roasted, baked, or boiled (para. 9)
> of curing the expensiveness of pride, vanity, idleness, and gaming in our women (para. 29)
> equally innocent, cheap, easy, and effectual (para. 32)
> by advancing our trade, providing for infants, relieving the poor, and giving pleasure to the rich (para. 33) [7]

What is observable about the proposer's amplifications is that his epithets are rarely just synonymous variations, such as the displays of *copia* that were common in Anglo-Saxon poetry and Euphuistic prose. In a phrase like "innocent, cheap, easy, and effectual," each adjective adds a distinct idea to the predication.

Along with this heavy compounding, Swift occasionally uses the scheme of polysyndeton—e.g. "in the arms or on the back or at the heels" (para. 2); "dying and rotting by cold and famine and filth and vermin" (para. 19). Multiplying conjunctions like this has the effect of further stringing out the list. Swift sometimes adds to the compounded elements the scheme of alliteration, as in the just-quoted "famine and filth and vermin" or in the triplet "parsimony, prudence, and temperance" (para. 29). In these examples, we get the impression of a man who is beginning to play with words. In the only other conspicuous use of alliteration, "in joints from the gibbet" (para. 18), our impulse to laugh at this sporting with words is suddenly restrained by our realization of the horror of the image. At

---

[7] There is nothing in *A Modest Proposal* that approaches the crushing catalogue of words in Book IV of *Gulliver's Travels*: "Hence it follows of necessity that the vast numbers of our people are compelled to seek their livelihood by begging, robbing, stealing, cheating, pimping, forswearing, flattering, suborning, forging, gaming, lying, fawning, hectoring, voting, scribbling, star-gazing, poisoning, whoring, canting, libelling, free-thinking, and the like occupations."

other times, Swift will reinforce the compounding with the scheme
/116/of climax, as in the two or three examples in the first paragraph
of the essay, or with the scheme of anti-climax, as in the example
quoted above from paragraph 33.

Although all of this compounding is done within the framework
of parallelism, parallelism is not a characteristic of the proposer's
style or of Swift's style in general. But Swift demonstrates that he
knows how and when to use parallel structure. In paragraph 29, the
key paragraph of the essay, he lays out his long enumeration of
"other expedients" on a frame of parallel structure. The list is long,
the list is important, and Swift wants to make sure that his readers
do not get lost in this maze of coordinate proposals.

Another thing that the long rambling sentences and the frequent
compounding might suggest is a "spoken" style. If one compares
spoken style with written style, one notes that spoken style tends to
be paratactic—a stitching together of coordinate units. We have just
observed this kind of rhapsodic structure in the word and phrase
units of *A Modest Proposal,* but when we look at the kinds of grammatical sentences (see Appendix), we observe a marked predomi-
nance of the subordinate structures that typify a sophisticated written
style. Over half of the sentences are complex, and almost a third of
the sentences are compound-complex. Although there are five simple
sentences in the essay, there is not a single compound sentence, which
is the commonest structure in extemporaneous spoken discourse. So
although the essay may give the impression of a certain colloquial
ease, this impression is not being produced by the syntax of the sentences.

Further evidence of a calculated literary style is found in the proposer's inclination to periodic structure. As Walter J. Ong said in a
recent article on prose style, "Oral composition or grammatical structure is typically non-periodic, proceeding in the 'adding' style;
literary composition tends more to the periodic."[8] We see this periodic structure exemplified in a sentence like the first one of paragraph 4: "As to my own part, having turned my thoughts, for many
years, upon this important subject, and maturely weighed the several
schemes of other projectors, I have always found them grossly mistaken in their computations." No one *speaks* a sentence like that;
sentences like that are produced by someone who has time to plot
his sentences.

---

[8] Walter J. Ong, "Oral Residue in Tudor Prose Style," *PMLA,* LXXX (June,
1965), 149.

This tendency to delay the main predication of the sentence is most pronounced within another structural pattern that is so common in the essay as to be a mannerism. I refer to the proposer's habit of putting the main idea of the sentence into a noun clause following the verb of the main clause. These noun clauses follow either personal structures like "I am assured by our merchants that . . . ," "I have reckoned that . . . ," "he confessed that . . ." or impersonal structures /117/like "it is not improbable that . . ." and "it is very well known that . . . ." There are at least nineteen instances like these, where the main idea of the sentence is contained in the noun clause. And frequently the proposer further delays the main idea by making us read almost to the end of the noun clause before he gives us the main predication. A prime example of this is the final sentence of paragraph 18:

> Neither indeed can I deny, that if the same use were made of several plump young girls in this town, who, without one single groat to their fortunes, cannot stir abroad without a chair, and appear at the playhouse and assemblies in foreign fineries, which they will never pay for, the kingdom would not be the worse.

Reading a sentence like this, we wonder whether the man will ever get to the point, and in this case, when the point is finally reached, we find that it is deflatingly anti-climactic.

This tendency toward periodic structure is evidence not only of a deliberate written style but of a habit of the *persona* that suits Swift's rhetorical purpose. I suggested earlier that part of Swift's rhetorical strategy is to create a character who will, as it were, "sneak up" on the reader. The frequent use of periodic structure is one of the ways in which the proposer "sneaks up" on the reader.

And we see this same tactic in the early paragraphs of the essay. In the first two paragraphs we see the long, leisurely, meandering sentences in which the proposer, in a matter-of-fact tone, describes the present condition of the poor. There is further dawdling in paragraph 4, where in two rambling sentences he seeks to establish his credentials with his audience. Then in paragraph 6, the second longest paragraph of the essay, we are subjected to a litany of cold, hard figures or "computations." In the short paragraph 9, we hear the disturbing sputter of a lighted fuse as the proposer details the testimony of his American acquaintance about what a delicacy a year-old child is. Then in paragraph 10, after the expenditure of almost a thousand words on preliminaries (almost a third of the essay), the proposer drops his bombshell. Nor does his pace become any more frenetic from this point on. He continues to "leak out" information, testimony, and arguments.

The noticeable periodic structure of many of the sentences, then, is part of Swift's strategy of sneaking up on the audience, of disarming the reader in order to render him more sensitive to the blow that will be delivered to the solar plexus. The proposer tells us in paragraph 27 that he is "studious of brevity." But he is not brief at all; he takes his own good time about dealing out what he has to say to his audience. This is not the curt Senecan amble; this is the ramb-/118/ ling Ciceronian cadence. The Ciceronian cadence does not fit Jonathan Swift, of course, but it does fit the character he has created and does contribute to the rhetorical effectiveness of the essay.

We could pursue this discussion of sentences and schemes, but let us move on to a consideration of the diction of the essay. Let us see what a study of the diction tells us about Swift's strategies and about the proposer's style.

To begin with, we might advert briefly to the words and idioms that mark the essay as a product of the eighteenth century. One of the things that has often been remarked of Swift's style is that it is strikingly modern. As one of my students said to me. "When I'm reading Swift, I have the feeling that I'm reading George Orwell all over again." One of the reasons certainly for this impression of modernity is the diction and idiom. Swift uses very few words and idioms that are outdated. But he does use just enough dated words and expressions to prevent our getting the impression that we are reading the morning newspaper. I counted about a dozen idioms which were peculiar to the eighteenth century or were still current in the eighteenth century but are no longer current—expressions like "of towardly parts" (para. 6), "no gentleman would *repine* to give ten shillings" (para. 14), "I cannot be altogether *in* his sentiments" (para. 17) (see Appendix for additional examples). If one were attempting to date this piece from internal evidence, probably the two words that would be the best index of the period in which this essay was written would be *shambles* (para. 16) and the *chair* (para. 18) in which the plump young girls ride about town. The *OED* would tell us that in the eighteenth century *shambles* meant "a place where meat is sold," "a slaughter house" and that *chair* designated a means of transportation. Expressions like these give the essay its Augustan flavor, but aside from these, the diction and idiom are remarkably modern.

The Appendix carries a note about the monosyllabism of the essay. Only about one-third of the nouns in the first ten paragraphs are monosyllabic, and I suspect that there is a much higher percentage of polysyllabic, Latinate diction in *A Modest Proposal* than we will find in most of Swift's other prose works, especially in that prose where he is speaking in his own voice. This polysyllabic diction is appropriate of course for the kind of pedantic character that Swift has created in *A Modest Proposal*. The proposer wants to pass himself off on his audience as a man who has indulged in a great deal of scientific, scholarly study of the problem, so as to enhance his authority—"having turned my thoughts, for many years, upon this important subject, and maturely weighed the several schemes of other projectors" (para. 4).

The mathematical and mercantile terminology is also contributing /119/to the image of the dedicated investigator and the political arithmetician. Besides the many figures cited, there are repeated uses of words like "compute," "reckon," "calculate," "shillings," "pounds," "sterling," "accounts," "stock," "commodity," "*per annum*." By putting jargon like this in the mouth of his proposer, Swift is making him talk the language of the other political economists who had turned their attention to the problem. We might say of the cold-bloodedness with which the proposer delivers himself of these terms that it represents his disinterested endeavor to propagate the worst that is known and thought about the problem in the Anglo-Irish world.

The most notable of the lexical means that Swift uses to achieve his purpose is the series of animal metaphors (see the Appendix). Charles Beaumont has pointed out that Swift is here employing the ancient rhetorical device of diminution, the opposite effect of amplification.[9] Swift first reduces his human beings to the status of animals and then to the status of food furnished to the table when these animals are slaughtered. So we pass from animal images like "dropped from its dam" and "reserved for breed" to such slaughtered-animal images as "the carcass," "the fore or hind quarters," and "the skin of which, artificially dressed." We feel the impact of these metaphors when we realize that Swift is suggesting that the Anglo-Irish landlords were treating human beings no better than they treated their

---

[9] See Charles Allen Beaumont, "A Modest Proposal," *Swift's Classical Rhetoric* (Athens, Ga.: University of Georgia Press, 1961), pp. 15-43. After my own gathering of data, it was reassuring to me to discover that I had noted many of the same stylistic features that Beaumont had found.

domestic animals. The proposer points up this inhuman treatment when he says, in paragraph 26, that if his proposal were adopted, "men would become as fond of their wives, during the time of pregnancy, as they are now of their mares in foal, their cows in calf, or sows when they are ready to farrow."

Another trope that Swift uses to achieve diminution is litotes—the opposite trope to hyperbole. Here are four prominent examples of litotes or understatement. In paragraph 2, the proposer refers to the burden of the prodigious number of beggar children as "a very great additional grievance." In paragraph 17, he speaks of the practice of substituting the bodies of young lads and maidens for venison as "a little bordering on cruelty." At the end of the periodic sentence in paragraph 18, he says that "the kingdom would not be the worse" if the bodies of plump young girls were sold as a delicacy for the table. The most notable example of litotes in the essay — and the one that serves as the chief tip-off to the irony of the essay—is found in the first sentence of the key paragraph 29: "I can think of no one objection that will possibly be raised against this proposal, unless it should be urged that the number of people will be thereby much lessened in this kingdom." The frequent use of litotes fits in well with the proposer's tendency to underplay everything.

The proposer not only underplays his proposal (note "a modest proposal") and his arguments to justify the proposal but also under-/120/plays his emotions. One has a hard time of it finding emotionally freighted words in the essay. Only in paragraphs 1 and 5 do I find conspicuous clusters of what I. A. Richards calls "emotive words":

  paragraph 1: Melancholy, all in rags, helpless infants, dear
    native country, crowded
  paragraph 5: abortions, horrid practice, murdering their bastard
    children, alas, tears and pity, poor innocent babes, savage
    and inhuman breast

The only other place in the essay where I sense the proposer losing a tight rein on his emotions is in his outburst in paragraph 18 against the plump young girls of the town, and in this instance, the anger simmering under these words is, I suspect, the emotional reaction of the clergyman Swift rather than of the worldly proposer. And this is the one place in the essay where I feel that Swift momentarily drops the mask and speaks in his own voice.

Swift considerably enhances the emotional impact of his message by this underplaying. And the other trope that is responsible for the emotional power of the essay is irony. As I remarked before, irony is an over-arching device for the entire essay: the proposer means what he says, but Swift does not. Irony, however, is a prevalent device within the essay too. I counted at least fifteen instances of words being used ironically. Rather than weary you with the entire catalogue, let me quote a few representative examples (the ironical words are italicized):

> will make two dishes at an *entertainment* for friends (para. 10)
> the fore and hind quarters will make a *reasonable* dish (para. 10)
> will make admirable gloves for *ladies* and summer boots for *fine gentlemen* (para. 14)
> some *scrupulous* people might be apt to censure (para. 17)

The horror of this irony hits us all the harder when we realize that the proposer, in his naivety, intends his words to be taken literally. These are the places where I can almost see Swift grinning through the lines of print.

Swift does something with words in this essay that I had not noticed him doing in any of his other prose works. He repeats key words so that they almost become motifs in the essay. The Appendix lists some of these repeated words and records the frequency of repetition. Note particularly the repetitions and variations of the words *child* and *parent*. Swift realizes that the proposal violates one of the most fundamental of human relations—the child-parent relation. When this violation of the normal child-parent relation is joined /121/with a suggestion of cannibalism, a practice that almost universally offends the sensibilities of mankind, we get a proposal of the utmost monstrosity. And if Swift can get his audience to react violently enough to the revolting proposal, there is hope that they will resort to some of the "other expedients" for a solution to the problem of poverty. Basically that is his main rhetorical strategy in the essay.

I cannot wholly account for the rhetorical function of the repetition of the kingdom-country-nation diction. Swift may be seeking to emphasize that the poverty of the people is a problem of national scope, one in which the welfare of the entire nation is crucially involved. Hasn't this been the theme that President Johnson has been urging in his efforts to promote his Poverty Program? Another explanation may be that Swift is suggesting that just as, on the domestic level, the normal child-parent relationships have broken down, the kingdom-citizen relationships have broken down on the national level.

This kind of repetition of key words and phrases is a device that we have come to associate with Matthew Arnold's style. Anyone who has read Arnold's prose extensively knows how effective this tactic can be for purposes of exposition. Although repetition is not a mannerism of Swift's style in general, we can appreciate the emotional effect that Swift achieves in this argumentative piece with these drumbeat repetitions. These insistent repetitions keep bringing us back to the full implications of the modest proposal.

Before this exhaustive analysis becomes prostratingly exhausting, I had better bring it to a quick conclusion. Maybe a good way to conclude this study is for me to quote two estimates of Swift's style and then to ask you which of these two estimates seems to be, in the light of the foregoing analysis, the more just.

The first quotation is from Dr. Johnson's *Life of Swift:*

> For purposes merely didactic, when something is to be told that was not known before [his style] is in the highest degree proper, but against that inattention by which known truths are suffered to lie neglected, it makes no provision; it instructs, but does not persuade.

There is no denying that Swift's style does achieve an "easy and safe conveyance of meaning," but do you find Dr. Johnson's denial of persuasive value in Swift's style too harsh? Perhaps you are more disposed to accept Coleridge's judgment on Swift's style: "The manner is a complete expression of the matter, the terms appropriate, and the artifice concealed."

But maybe it is unfair to ask you to choose between these two estimates, for one of my points has been that in this essay we are observing not so much Swift's style as a style that Swift has created for/122/ his modest proposer. And who, after all, remembers this essay for its style? This analysis has revealed, I hope, that there is considerable stylistic artifice in *A Modest Proposal*, but hasn't this essay become memorable mainly because of the monstrousness of the proposal and the cleverness of the ironical form? As a matter of historical fact, Swift did *not* succeed in persuading his audience to do something about a lamentable situation. But he did succeed in producing a great piece of literature.

Appendix

Some Statistics on Swift's *A Modest Proposal*

3474 words
  33 paragraphs
  61 sentences   (For this study, a sentence is defined as a group of words beginning with a capital letter and ending with some mark of terminal punctuation.)

Average number of words per paragraph ⸻ 105.2
Average number of sentences per paragraph ⸻ 1.84
    18 one-sentence paragraphs
    7 two-sentence paragraphs
    4 three-sentence paragraphs
    3 four-sentence paragraphs
    1 five-sentence paragraph (#29)
Shortest paragraph #8 (20 words)—a transitional paragraph (other
    transitional paragraph, #20, is 34 words long)
Longest paragraph #29 (289 words) — "other expedients" (a key
    paragraph)
Average number of words per sentence ⸻ 56.9
Number of sentences 10 words or more *above* average ⸻ 18
Percentage of sentences above average ⸻ 29.5%
Number of sentences 10 words or more *below* average ⸻ 28
Percentage of sentences below average ⸻ 45.9%
Longest sentence ⸻ 179 words (para. 32)
Other long sentences: 164 words (para. 6) ; 141 words (para. 29) ; 119
    words (para. 18) ; 109 words (para. 4) ; 102 words (para. 13)
Shortest sentence ⸻ 11 words (last sentence of para. 27)
    (other short sentence: first sentence of transitional paragraph
    #20)
34 Complex sentences
18 Compound-complex sentences
  5 Simple sentences (paragraphs 4, 19, 20, 27)
  4 Elliptical or incomplete sentences (paragraphs 10, 29 (two), 31)

Repeated Words

child (children) ⸻25 ⎫
infants ⸻6 ⎬ ⸻33
babes ⸻2 ⎭

kingdom ⸻13 ⎫
country ⸻9 ⎬ ⸻27
nation ⸻5 ⎭

/123/

mother ⸻6 ⎫
parents ⸻7 ⎬ ⸻20
breed (breeders) ⸻7 ⎭

the year ⸻6 ⎫
one year old ⸻1 ⎪
annually ⸻3 ⎬ ⸻16
solar year ⸻2 ⎪
per annum ⸻4 ⎭

number ⸻7 ⎫
compute ⸻5 ⎬ ⸻15
reckon ⸻2 ⎪
calculate ⸻1 ⎭

food ⸻7 ⎫
flesh ⸻4 ⎪
carcass ⸻5 ⎬ ⸻19
plump ⸻3 ⎭

propose ⸻5 ⎫ ⸻9
proposal ⸻4 ⎭

gentlemen ⸻5 ⎫
persons of quality ⸻2 ⎬ ⸻12
beggars ⸻5 ⎭

Swift's *A Modest Proposal*

Diction or idiom peculiarly eighteenth-century

(The number in parentheses refers to the paragraph in which the expression occurs.)

(6) of *towardly* parts
(10) increas*eth* to twenty-eight pounds
(13) fish being a *prolific* diet
(14) no gentleman would *repine* to give ten shillings
(16) *shambles* may be appointed
(16) dressing them hot from the knife
(17) the *want* of venison . . . for *want* of work and service
(17) I cannot be altogether *in* his sentiments
(18) who came from *thence, above* twenty years ago
(18) without a *chair*
(19) and I have been desired to employ my thoughts what course may be taken
(19) But I am not *in the least pain upon* that matter
(19) and thus the country and themselves are *in a fair way* of being delivered from the evils to come
(25) bring great *custom* to taverns where the *vintners* will certainly be so prudent
(26) emulation among the married women, *which* of them could bring
(32) to reject any offer, proposed by wise men, *who* [which?] shall be found equally innocent, cheap, easy, and effectual

Animal Imagery

(3) at the *heels* of their mother
(4) a child just *dropped* from its *dam*
(10) reserved for breed
(10) more than we allow to sheep, black-cattle, or swine
(10) therefore one *male* will be sufficient to *serve* four *females*
(10) to let them *suck* plentifully...to render them plump and fat for a good table
(10) the fore or hind quarter/124/
(14) for the *carcass* of a good fat child
(15) flay the *carcass* . . . the skin of which, artificially *dressed*
(16) as we do roasting pigs
(26) men would become as fond of their wives, during the time of their pregnancy, as they are now of their mares in foal, their cows in calf, or sows when they are ready to farrow
(27) propagation of swine's flesh
(27) the great destruction of pigs
(27) fat *yearling* child

Monosyllabism

In the first ten paragraphs of the essay, there are 1127 words; of these, (60%) 685 are monosyllabic. But since a good many of these monosyllabic words are pronouns, prepositions, conjunctions, or auxiliary verbs, we get an unreliable estimate of Swift's diction. If we look at the nouns only, we get a different picture. In these same ten paragraphs, there are only 204 nouns. Of these, 73 are monosyllabic (36%), 131 are polysyllabic. If we regard only the substantive words in these paragraphs, we get, for Swift, an unusually high number of polysyllabic words.

Charles Beaumont

The Classical Rhetoric of
"A Modest Proposal"*

Swift's best and most popular ironical essay, "A Modest Proposal," reveals Swift at once as master ironist and master classical rhetorician. In investigating the various elements of classical rhetoric employed in this essay and indicating how each functions either within the irony or to build the irony, I will explore the following major topics: the classical form of the essay; the ethical proof; the use of the two major rhetorical devices, diminution and refining; and the less frequently used devices.

The Classical Form

The essay is organized in the manner of a classical oration, as follows:

Exordium	----	Paragraphs	1	through	7
Narration	----	Paragraphs	8	through	16
Digression	----	Paragraphs	17	through	19
Proof	----	Paragraphs	20	through	28
Refutation	----	Paragraphs	29	through	30
Peroration	----	Paragraphs	31	through	33

The exordium includes three kinds of material, all of which are acceptable in a classical exordium: a pitiful description of the state of Ireland, intended to appeal to the emotions of the reader; statements which reflect the benevolence of the author, designed to establish the

---

*Reprinted from Charles A. Beaumont, *Swift's Classical Rhetoric* (Athens: The University of Georgia Press, 1961), pp. 15-43, by permission of the publisher. Copyright 1961 by the University of Georgia Press.

ethical proof; and hints and preparatory statements for the proof to follow.

The narration contains the statement of the proposal, with some further preparation for the proof.

Instead of going immediately into the proof, the projector inserts, in good classical form, a digression. Its subject matter/16/parallels the subject matter of the essay by relating the custom of the Formosan court in eating the flesh of young girls whose bodies have just been cut down by the public hangman.

Following this digression containing the historical parallel is the proof, which contains six major reasons why the proposal should be accepted, plus the several summarized reasons.

In the refutation the projector brushes aside the single objection which he feels can reasonably be urged against him, that the population would be greatly decreased. He incorporates this argument into his own, claiming that it was one of his chief motives. He also sweeps aside the vain, visionary, and foolish "expedients" which have been offered in the past.

The peroration is made up of further statements which reflect favourably on the character of the projector and of a reiteration of the major topics of the essay. The appeal to the emotions stops one paragraph short of the end of the peroration. Just as Swift regularly undercuts a sentence with a fine irony at the end of the sentence, so he concludes the whole essay with a subdued minor point which is almost an ironic aside: in this case, his personal reference to the fact that his wife is past child-bearing.

The classical form of the essay is itself an important constituent of Swift's irony, for the projector's addressing his readers through an ancient and learned form helps to allay any suspicion of radical newness. A revolutionary new proposal is insinuated in a traditional, respected form.

The Ethical Proof

The moral and ethical character of the pleader is one of the three major proofs designated by Aristotle.[1] This kind of proof is one of the

---

[1] Aristotle divides all proof into two areas: inartificial (the facts which exist) and artificial (the use made of the facts through the art of rhetoric). He divides artificial proof into three kinds: ethical, emotional, and logical. The ethical proof stems from the moral character of the pleader himself (*Rhet.* I.ii.3). Quintilian agrees: although the pleader "may be modest and say little about himself, yet if he is believed to be a good man, this consideration will exercise the strongest influ-

main kinds employed by Swift in most of his satires and much of his other writing (especially in his role as Examiner). In varying degrees, every essay by him which has an "author" makes use of this kind of classical proof. The sources of this proof in any oration are two: the implicit indications of the moral character of the pleader and the explicit ones. The implicit ones are made up of the whole tone of the essay and are not to be isolated. The explicit ones are the overt indications throughout the speech. Swift has made use of his exordium to begin the explicit/17/characterization by showing the projector's concern, compassion, and high motive in modestly suggesting this beneficial solution to the state of Ireland. This establishing the character and motives of the pleader is a standard use of the classical exordium.

The specific details by which Swift builds up the ethical proof fall into four categories descriptive of the projector: his humanity, his self-confidence, his competence in the immediate subject of the proposal, and his reasonableness.

The humanity of the projector is immediately revealed in the opening words of the address. While the projector is moving his audience to pity with his description of the "melancholy Object of those, who walk through the streets of this great Town," he is also indicating the humane inclinations of the speaker, who is also capable of being moved to such pity.

In the proof the projector reflects his compassion for the "poorer Tenants" who "will have something valuable of their own" if the proposal is put into effect. Later in the same section (paragraph 26) he cites as a reason for his proposal the kind and humane treatment it would assure expectant mothers, as well as its tendency to increase "the Care and Tenderness of Mothers toward their Children."

In the digression (paragraph 17) the projector objects to the proffered "Refinement" on his proposal (that young lads and maidens be used in place of venison) because "some scrupulous People might be apt to censure such a Practice (although indeed very unjustly) as a little bordering upon Cruelty; which, I confess, hath always been with me the strongest Objection against any Project, how well soever in-

---

ence at every point in the case. For thus he will have the good fortune to give the impression not so much that he is a zealous advocate as that he is an absolutely reliable witness. It is therefore pre-eminently desirable that he should be believed to have undertaken the case out of a sense of duty, by a sense of patriotism or at any rate some serious moral consideration" (*Instit.* IV.i.7.). The texts I have used are those of the Loeb Classical Library. *The Art of Rhetoric,* Tr. John Henry Freeze (London: William Heinemann, Ltd., 1947) and *Institutio Oratoria,* Tr. H. E. Butler (London, 1953).

tended." In the litotes "a little bordering upon Cruelty" the projector accomplishes several purposes. He indicates his own humaneness in rejecting this refinement partially on grounds of cruelty. He gains an argumentative point by branding all other proposals as cruel also. Notice that he does not explicitly exclude his own proposal when he says, "which, I confess hath always been with me the strongest Objection against *any* Project." (Italics mine.) However, he recoups this hint of concession by observing that such an objection stems from too nice a scrupulosity./18/

In the last paragraph he assures the reader of his great sincerity and unselfish motives: "I PROFESS, in the Sincerity of my Heart, that I have not the least personal Interest, in endeavouring to promote this necessary Work. . . . I have no Children, by which I can propose to get a single Penny; the youngest being nine Years old, and my Wife past Childbearing." This last sentence gives two more pieces of information which are important to the character of the pleader. He is not a childless man who can propose such a solution in ignorance of a father's feelings, and he will not gain personally from the adoption of the proposal.

Because the projector of this proposal is sometimes thought of as the *ingénu* type, a somewhat diffident, inexperienced person who has come upon the scene without being in complete touch with the whole situation, it has not been sufficiently noticed that he is at the same time a bit cocksure.[2] In creating his projector, Swift faced a rhetorical problem that required the careful balancing of these rather contrasting characteristics in one person. He had to make the projector humble enough to gain the reader's approval and sympathy and confident enough to gain the reader's confidence in his ability and qualifications with the subject.[3] Added to this double problem is the fact that, while both of these ends were being accomplished, the projector had to be kept sufficiently dense to sustain the irony.

The self-confidence of the projector is first indicated in the second paragraph, in which, a bit presumptuously, he looks forward to seeing himself commemorated with a statue for being "a Preserver of the Nation." His sureness of himself and of the efficacy of his proposal is

---

[2] A pleader must reflect self-confidence in himself and in his own proposals if he expects his audience to be convinced. The classical rhetoricians agree that the best delivery is that in which the pleader either participates in or seems to participate in the emotions and convictions which he is displaying.

[3] Quintilian *Instit.* VI.ii.26.: "The prime essential for stirring the emotions of others is, in my opinion, first to feel these emotions oneself." See also Cicero *De Oratore* II.xlv.189.

stated in a qualified form in the opening sentence of the narration: "I SHALL NOW therefore humbly propose my own Thoughts; which I hope will not be liable to the least Objection," and is echoed in the first sentence of the refutation: "I CAN think of no one Objection, that will possibly be raised against this Proposal; unless it should be urged, that the Number of People will be thereby much lessened in the Kingdom." This last, concessive clause is quickly done away with by the author's turning this single objection into an advantage for his cause.[4]

A pleader in the act of refuting naturally shows self-con-/19/fidence. So does the projector when he tells us of his friend's suggesting that the lack of venison could be supplied by the youth of Ireland.

In paragraph nineteen the projector stands in contrast to "SOME Persons of desponding Spirit" who are in as great a concern for the aged as he is for the youth. He asserts that he is "not in the least Pain upon that matter": one could not reasonably expect the aged to be taken care of any more rapidly than they are by death, famine, and the like.

The projector speaks out boldly in introducing his proof: "I think the Advantages by the Proposal which I have made are obvious, and many, as well as of the highest Importance." And he proceeds to list and describe six of these advantages, but finally (implying that there are too many advantages to list) he summarizes the rest. Argument from a wealth of reasons indicates the firmness of the projector's position, since he can afford to waste them.

Closely related to the self-confidence of the pleader is his competence in dealing with the subject at hand. The projector gives abundant evidence that he is capable of dealing with the problem. First, he has not burst into print without first giving much thought and research to this problem: "As to my own Part, having turned my

---

[4] Decreasing the population of Ireland would, as the projector views the problem, improve the situation by lessening the number of people to be fed and otherwise maintained. But, the projector continues, this proposal is calculated *"for this one individual Kingdom of* IRELAND, *and for no other that ever was, is, or I think ever can be upon Earth."* Landa points out that an argument which recurs in Swift's Irish tracts is that, because the situation in Ireland is so pitifully unique, the best maxims on government and economics cannot operate there. Swift seems to have accepted the mercantile concept that the people are the wealth of a nation and that prosperity is dependent upon a constantly increasing population. (See Louis A. Landa, *"A Modest Proposal* and Populousness," *MP,* XL (Nov., 1942), pp. 161-70.) The projector's statement is an ironical inversion of the maxim. Also, of course, Swift is making use of the maxim by rendering it literal: in "A Modest Proposal" the infants are literally to be the wealth of the nation.

Thoughts for many Years, upon this important Subject, and maturely weighed the several *Schemes of other Projectors*, I have always found them grosly mistaken in their Computation." He then plunges into a barrage of mathematical calculations, which of course indicate his painstaking work and thought on the subject. In paragraph six he begins with the figure of 200,000 couples, from which he subtracts 30,000 who can maintain their own children. He subtracts 50,000 more couples whose children will not live. This leaves 120,000 couples to be provided for. In the next two sentences he states

> I again subtract Fifty Thousand, for those Women who miscarry, or whose Children die by Accident, or Disease, within the Year. There only remain an Hundred and Twenty Thousand Children of poor Parents, annually born. . . .

The projector returns to the idea in paragraph ten: "the Hundred and Twenty Thousand Children, already computed. . . ." He subtracts 20,000 more children who are to be pre-/20/served for breeding, only one-fourth of these to be males.[5] It is this solid core of mathematics which makes the proposal so real and so practical—such a "fair, cheap, and easy Method."

This competence in calculations is reinforced by the vocabulary of the essay: "I HAVE reckoned upon a Medium. . . ." "As to our City of *Dublin;* Shambles may be appointed for this Purpose. . . ." "SUPPOSING that one Thousand Families in this City, . . . I compute. . . ."

In addition to such verbal indicants of competence, the whole movement of the proof reflects the strong debater arguing from a wealth of material. Six carefully thought out advantages are brought forward in such a way as to imply that he could continue listing advantages indefinitely, but finally he stops, being (as he says) "studious of Brevity." His two large rhetorical questions in paragraph thirty-two which he poses to his would-be answerers complement this listing by indicating movingly and thoroughly the consequence which will obtain if the proposal is not accepted. Thus, both through the careful attention to the smallest detail and through the marshalling of the whole movement of the essay, Swift has succeeded in creating an aura of rightness in the carefully thought out and convincingly presented proposal.

---

[5] Swift seems here to be satirizing the economic projectors, whose pamphlets abound in mazes of mathematics. See George Wittkowsky, "Swift's 'Modest Proposal'; the Biography of an Early Georgian Pamphlet," *Journal of the History of Ideas,* IV (Jan., 1943), pp. 75-104.

The reasonableness of the pleader, the fourth heading under which the character of the projector is established, is amply provided for by Swift. A reference already cited in another connection is also to the point here: "as to my own Part, having turned my Thoughts for many years, upon this important Subject. . . ." This careful deliberation suggests a reasonable rather than a rash pleader. "AFTER all, I am not so violently bent upon my own Opinion, as to reject any Offer proposed by wise Men, which shall be found equally cheap, easy, and effectual."

The projector reflects his reasonableness by the conservative nature of his calculations. In establishing 30,000 as the number of couples who can maintain their own children, he says, "although I apprehend there cannot be so many, *under the present Distresses of the Kingdom.* . . ."

Concession occurs again in the same paragraph.[6] The projector states that children under six are seldom good thieves,/21/"although, I must confess, they learn the Rudiments [of stealing] much earlier."

In allowing that of the 20,000 reserved for breeders, only one-fourth will be males, the projector through concession emphasizes the generosity of his calculation, for this proportion "is more than we allow to *Sheep, black Cattle,* or *Swine.*"

The projector, in declining the "worthy Person's" refinement on his scheme (that the bodies of young lads and maidens between the ages of twelve and fourteen could be used for venison), concedes that there would be a slight chance for cruelty, "which, I confess, hath always been with me the strongest Objection against any Project, how well soever intended."

In describing the Formosan practice of court ministers' buying the bodies of young girls fresh from the gibbet, the projector concedes, "Neither indeed can I deny, that if the same Use were made of several plump young girls of the Town" the kingdom might be better off.

Most of these concessions are of little importance to the projector's central argument, but their use, where they cannot damage the proposition, tends to create an impression in the reader of the projector's reasonableness and lack of dogmatism.

Closely associated with this device of concession is that of deference to superiors (a device greatly needed in the Roman courts of the Empire, especially when an important or powerful personage had to

---

[6] I have here used the name *concession* for this device. Quintilian discusses concession, confession, and agreement as allied figures "which have a strong family resemblance." All three are used to concede points "that can do our case no harm." The act of concession implies a strong, confident position. (*Instit.* IX.ii.51-52.).

be attacked but attacked politely). The projector graciously defers to the "worthy Person" who had offered a refinement on his scheme. "But with due Deference to so excellent a Friend, and so deserving a Patriot, I cannot be altogether in his Sentiments." Such use of the young girls would be wasteful because they soon would become producers of this new food: "Then, as to the Females, it would, I think, with humble Submission, *be a Loss to the Public*, because they soon would become Breeders themselves. . . ."

Actually, of course, the projector concedes nothing; neither does he really defer to anyone. However, a tone of concession and of deference is present and contributes to the ethical proof.

I have said that the projector is a bit cocksure. He is also/22/ manifestly humble and modest. The proposal is a "modest" one. It is introduced in generally modest terms: "I SHALL NOW therefore humbly propose my own Thoughts . . ."; "I do humbly offer to *publick Consideration.* . . ." Swift has blended these two qualities of his projector in such a way that both are convincing and that neither quality overshadows the other. The result is a pleader whose humility is justifiably tempered by the sure knowledge that he has something to offer Ireland, to her everlasting benefit.

These are the explicit indicants of the moral character of the pleader; they are reinforced and dramatized by the whole tone of the essay. From this stable personality Swift allows only one outburst of real anger and pathos. It occurs at the climax of the essay, when the patient but exhausted old projector, "having been wearied out for many Years with offering vain, idle, visionary Thoughts," turns in righteous indignation to insist: "THEREFORE I repeat, let no Man talk to me of these and the like Expedients; till he hath, at least, a Glimpse of Hope, that there will ever be some hearty and sincere Attempt to put *them in Practice.*"

Diminution

The principle of diminution is the informing device of the entire essay; it underlies the whole animal motif. This diminution of man to animal Quintana sees in its perfected form in Book IV of *Gulliver's Travels* and in "A Modest Proposal." It is, he says, perhaps "the most devastating weapon ever used by a satirist."[7]

---

[7] Ricardo Quintana, *The Mind and Art of Jonathan Swift* (Oxford: The University Press, 1936), p. 43. Several of the examples of diminution partake also of comparison; but, since diminution is the broader term for this particular context, all those examples of comparison will be considered in this section.

Swift's use of the device of diminution will be found to take three general directions, the first being the most pervasive: the creation of the illusion of animality, the substitution of the lesser word, and the imputation of the lesser motive.

The most obvious form of diminution is the use of the lesser noun to refer to people — especially to mothers and fathers. Strolling mothers are *"Beggars* of the female Sex." As if speaking of any mammal, the projector comments that "It is true a Child, *just dropped from its Dam,* may be supported by her Milk for a solar Year with little other Nourishment. . . ." In the mathematical working out of how many/23/babies to save, the projector refers to the couples merely as "Breeders."[8] Only a fourth part of these "breeders" are to be male "which is more than we allow to *Sheep, black Cattle,* or *Swine. . . .*" Like other animals, the mother will be able to work "until she produceth another Child."

As there are certain seasons when most animals foal, the projector with the help of a grave author finds that the human animals will produce most in December and January. He reckons that the markets will be most glutted a year after Lent.[9]

There will be no lack of people willing to set up butchery shambles in Dublin; however, "I rather recommend buying the Children alive, and dressing them hot from the Knife, as we do *roasting Pigs.*" The *"true Lover of his Country"* has suggested that, "many fine Gentlemen of this Kingdom, having of late destroyed their Deer," "the Want of Venison might well be supplied by the Bodies of young Lads and Maidens, not exceeding fourteen Years of Age or under Twelve."

As if referring to cattle, the projector calculates that since the cost of maintaining 100,000 children after the age of two can be estimated at not less than ten shillings *per annum,* "the nation's Stock will be thereby increased Fifty Thousand Pounds *per annum.* . . ." (There is here a pun upon stock as livestock, as financial stock, and as pantry stock.)

---

[8] In addition to this terminology's function in the animal diminution, it also satirizes the economic projector who is wont to deal with people as if they were only statistics, or as if they were cattle.

[9] The projector states, "I have reckoned upon a Medium, that a Child just born will weigh Twelve Pounds. . . ." The very grossness of the figure *12* suggests that it is a part of the animal diminution and is to be taken as an inhuman size for an *average* child at birth (for an average of 12 pounds requires some weights to be at least as high as 16 pounds). We should not, however, be too quick to apply mid-twentieth-century obstetrical standards to this figure. Only unavailable medical case histories of early 18th-century Ireland could prove the point. It is always possible that Swift simply did not know about such things, but if this be the case, it is the only instance in the whole essay which he has not investigated to the minutest detail.

"Men would become as *fond* of their Wives, during the time of their Pregnancy, as they are now of their *Mares* in Foal, their *Cows* in *Calf*, or *Sows* when they are ready to farrow. . . ." Beyond the equating the expectant mothers to animals, there is here the implication that men are humane to their animals and not to their wives.

Not only will a "well-grown fat yearling Child" well grace a Lord Mayor's feast, but also the projector can depend upon the pride of the women as to *"which of them could bring the fattest Child to the Market."* The "Customers of Infants Flesh" would in Dublin alone "take off, annually, about Twenty Thousand Carcasses; and the rest of the Kingdom (where probably they will be sold somewhat cheaper) the remaining Eighty Thousand."

At the beginning of the mathematical calculations the people were referred to as "souls," but at the end they have become "Creatures in human Figure," "Mouths and Backs."/24/

It is easy to get the impression from reading the essay casually that Swift creates the animal transfer by avoiding the use of terms appropriate to human beings. But this is not quite true. *Mother, father, child, children, babe, youth, lad, maiden, infant* are liberally sprinkled throughout the essay. With the exception of the word *carcass* (used in reference to children in paragraphs 15, 27, and 28) all of the other nouns applied to children are terms for food (see the next paragraph, below). In addition to the use of a lower term, Swift effects the animal diminution by juxtaposition of modifier and noun, as in "yearling Child." Rhetorically, the projector's constantly varying the normal term with the animal term serves to keep the reader off guard, with the result that if the reader begins to expect the animal term, he is fooled. The resulting effect is that one term is just as normal as the other. The animal terms are slipped in unobtrusively, and they are never insisted upon.

As if the diminution of human beings to animals were not strong enough, the irony is intensified by a species of redoubled diminution: the animal becomes food. The progression of diminution thus becomes man to animal to food (with the obvious implication that man is an animal to eat such food, or even worse than an animal, there being relatively few animals which are cannibalistic). Notice the final step in the diminution to food in the following statements. A "young healthy Child, well nursed, is, at a Year old, a most delicious, nourishing, and wholesome Food; whether *stewed, roasted, baked* or *boiled;* and I make no doubt, that it will equally serve in a *Fricasie,* or *Ragoust.*" They will be "plump and fat for a good Table. A Child will make two Dishes at an Entertainment for Friends; and when the family dines alone, the fore or hind Quarter will make a reasonable

Dish; and seasoned with a little Pepper or Salt, will be very good Boiled on the fourth Day, especially in *Winter*." One of Swift's most devastating techniques of word order is the final twist or insinuation with which he can charge the last phrase of a sentence. Witness the last phrase of the preceding sentence.

This new food will be "somewhat dear" and therefore "very *proper for Landlords*; who, as they have already *devoured* [italics mine] most of the Parents, seem to have the best Title to the Children."/25/

If such man-to-animal diminution stood alone in the essay, it would no doubt be so offensive that it would defeat its intended purpose of persuading the reader. However, as Swift has blended the operation of this device with the functioning of the several other devices, the whole resultant fabric of the irony is made so tight-knit that this particular use of diminution is one highly successful and basic to the whole essay. The steady reiteration of this diminution tends to establish it in the reader's consciousness as a norm, and thus the rhetorical device becomes one of the means of establishing the ironic norm of the essay. Obviously care had to be exercised not to overplay the device lest it boomerang. Swift so maniplates its use that by slipping in a word here and a phrase there, the impression of normalness (and the resultant acceptance) is gradually achieved.

All of the uses of diminution in this essay are not concerned directly with the animal figure, although, since the other uses of the device contribute to the dehumanizing tone of the whole essay, they can be said to contribute indirectly. The remaining uses are of two kinds: the use of the worse word to name a thing and the assumption of the worse motive in the performance of an act.

In paragraph two the "Children" in Ireland become "a very great additional Grievance." And in paragraph nineteen the old people are "a grievous. . . . Incumbrance." A mother can nourish her child for a solar year on as little as two shillings, "which the Mother may certainly get, or the Value in Scraps, by her lawful Occupation of *Begging*."

The proposal will prevent "those *voluntary Abortions*, and that horrid Practice of *Women murdering their Bastard Children*; alas! too frequent among us; sacrificing the *poor innocent Babes*, I doubt, more to avoid the Expence than the Shame; which would move Tears and Pity in the most Savage and inhuman Breast." There are two kinds of diminution in this sentence. The lesser motive is imputed when the projector states that the mothers will so act in order to avoid the expense rather than the shame, and animality is implied when the projector observes that such an act would move a savage or an inhuman breast to tears. The few casual references to savages, Laplanders, and the inhabitants of Topinamboo com-/26/bine to suggest to the reader that here are some people who might well be emulated. These references also provide a further standard by which the ironic norm can through contrast be brought into even sharper focus.

Swift's extensive use of diminution can be studied advantageously in tabular form. The following table presents a graphic summary of all of the nouns and a few of the verbs and modifiers which Swift has used in the diminution from man to animal, indicating the extent, the incidence, and the gradations of diminution.

PARENTS

Paragraph Number	Best Name	Impersonal or Less Name	Animal or Food Term
1	mothers	female sex	
2	mothers	beggars	
	fathers		
3	parents		
4	parents		dam
5		women	
6	wives	souls	breeders
		women	
	poor parents		
	parents		
10	mother		
12	parents		
14	mother	beggars	produceth another
		cottagers	child
		labourers	
		farmers	
		tenants	
17	parents	nearest	
		relations	breeders
19		females	
		aged, diseased, maimed poor people	
		young labourers/27/	
21		papists	breeders
		dangerous enemies	
		good protestants	
22		poor tenants	
24			constant breeders

PARENTS

Paragraph Number	Best Name	Impersonal or Less Name	Animal or Food Term
26	mothers	men	
	wives	married women	
29		women	
		shop-keepers	
32	parents	beggars	breed
	wives	beggars	
		cottagers	
		labourers	
33		the poor	

CHILDREN

Paragraph Number	Best Name	Impersonal or Less Name	Animal or Food Term
1	children		
	helpless		
	infants		
2	children	grievance	
	children		
3	children		
	infants		
4	child		just dropped from
5	innocent		dam
	babes	bastard children	
6	children		number
	children		probationary thieves
	children		
7	boy		
	girl		
9	child		wholesome food
10	children	males	for breed
	children	male	two dishes
	child	females	
11	child		
12	children/28/		
13		Papist infants	infant's flesh
14	child	beggar's child	carcass of a good fat child
			4 dishes of nutritive meat
15			carcass

CHILDREN

Paragraph Number	Best Name	Impersonal or Less Name	Animal or Food Term
16	children		bought alive & dressed hot, as we do pigs
17		bodies of lads and maidens both sexes males	for venison flesh
18		young person body of plump girl plump young girls	carcass a prime dainty
23	children		new dish goods
24	children		
25			food
26	children babes		fattest child at the market
27			carcasses fat well-grown yearling child
28			infant's flesh
29			carcasses
31			commodity flesh
32	children	mouths backs mortals	
33	infants children		

Swift refers to the parents by the best name sixteen times, by the impersonal name twenty-eight times, and by the animal name eight times. Naming them most frequently by the im-/29/personal middle term is consistent with his purpose of neutralizing these human beings so that, on the eight occasions of referring to them in animal terms, easy acceptance of the animal terms results. By firmly establishing the middle term, Swift has not had to make the broad jump from human being to animal; he moves only from the middle or neutral term to the animal term.

The acceptance of the parents as breeders of animals makes the acceptance of babies as animals much easier. Thus, by natural sequence, the parent-as-animal diminution serves as preparation for the babies-as-animals diminution. It further allows for the larger number of references to the children as animals and as food. Swift refers to the children by the best name twenty-nine times, by the impersonal name sixteen times, and by the animal name twenty-four times. The low incidence of the middle term in naming children results from the foundation laid by its high incidence in naming parents. (This balance results not from a chronological sequence in the essay but from the sequence in nature, that the offspring will naturally be like the parents.) Building the diminution carefully in this manner, Swift was free to push the terrible juxtaposition of the two extremes, the best name coupled with the animal or food name for children.

It is through observing and understanding each such careful handling by Swift of a particular device of rhetoric that one comes better to comprehend the full implications of Swift's rhetorical art and its contribution to his irony. Only thus can we begin to explain most readers' amazement reflected in the question, "How does he get away with rendering human beings as animals in a few brief paragraphs?" His painstaking manipulation of rhetoric supplies the answer.

Refining

Refining "consists in dwelling on the same topic and yet seeming to say something new."[10] It can be accomplished by a variation in words, in delivery, or in treatment (e.g., by a change in the form—to dialogue, to characterization, etc.). The device appears in Swift's essay; however, it is put to a much subtler use than the author of *Ad Herennium* had in mind. Swift's use of refining is akin to what Martin Price has/30/called "redefinition":[11] in referring to something, Swift varies the word until finally the word or phrase has a new meaning, a meaning which Swift intended it to have all along but which he carefully avoided expressing.

For example, the proposal is ostensibly designed for the children of professional beggars, who hardly make up a majority of the population. Swift must redefine "professional Beggar" so as to include all of the poor within this term. The pride of the poor is as great as the pride of the rich; therefore Swift eases the redefinition in by "refining" it, by varying the terms without seeming to dwell on them. This

---

[10] *Rhetorica ad Herennium*, tr. Harry Caplan (Loeb Classical Library; London: William Heinemann, Ltd., 1954), IV.xlii.54.

[11] Martin Price, *Swift's Rhetorical Art: A Study in Structure and Meaning* (New Haven: Yale University Press, 1953), pp. 27-31.

is accomplished in three steps and reinforced in a fourth (paragraphs 2, 3, 14, and 32, in that order). The pitiful strollers in paragraph one are said to be beggars (whether technically professional beggars is not made clear). In paragraph three the projector states, "BUT my Intention is very far from being confined to provide only for the Children of *professed Beggars:* It is of a much greater Extent, and shall take in the whole Number of Infants at a certain Age, who are born of Parents, in effect as little able to support them, as those who demand our Charity in the Streets." The two groups (the beggars and the poor) are put on one footing, but they remain two groups. In the next several paragraphs all of the mathematical calculations are concerned with "the Children of the Poor," beggars not being mentioned. Swift waits until paragraph fourteen to push the identification: "I HAVE already computed the Charge of nursing a Beggar's Child (in which List I reckon all *Cottagers, Labourers,* and Four fifths of the *Farmers*). . . ." The identification is complete, and it has been accomplished by a quite casual parenthesis. The word *beggar* is used only once again in the essay: in the peroration, where the projector states "adding those who are Beggars by profession, to the Bulk of Farmers, Cottagers, and Labourers, with their Wives and Children, who are Beggars in Effect." Through such refining Swift has steered a precarious course: he has made the identification of the poor and the beggars and at the same time he has refined so subtly that he has not impugned the dignity of the group in whose behalf he is writing.

But all of Swift's refining is not so gentle; neither is it aimed at redefinition. The landlords fare far worse. The word/31/*landlord* (or its equivalent "Gentleman of Fortune") occurs eleven times. The refining is merely verbal, and these words occur with iterative force to drive home the idea that the landlords will be the main eaters of this new food. This accusation against the landlords is prepared for in paragraphs six through ten, in which this new food is discussed. Who will eat it is only implied, until finally, late in paragraph ten, the projector states that these babies are to be "offered in Sale to *Persons of Quality* and *Fortune* through the Kingdom. . . ." The verb *offered* does not yet explicitly mean that these persons will accept the offer. Then in paragraph twelve the projector concedes that the food "will be somewhat dear, and therefore very *proper for Landlords;* who, as they have already devoured most of the Parents, seem to have the best Title to the Children." From this bold statement forward, the idea is not allowed to rest. In paragraph fourteen, it is repeated twice: "no Gentleman would repine to give Ten Shillings for the *Carcase of a good fat Child. . . .* thus the Squire will learn to be a good Landlord, and grow popular with his Tenants. . . ." In the next paragraph (15) we are told that the flayed carcasses will "make admirable *Gloves for Ladies*, and *Summer Boots for fine Gentlemen.*"

In the very next paragraph (16) the idea is implied in the discussion of the butchering of new food. And in the paragraph following (17), we meet the "VERY worthy person, *a true Lover of his Country*," "so excellent a Friend, and so deserving a Patriot" who sees a way to refine this modest proposal. This is followed in the next paragraph by the story of the usage of the Formosan court (with the parallel implied).

The refining continues in paragraph twenty-two: "SECONDLY, the poorer Tenants will have something valuable of their very own, which, by Law, may be made liable to Distress, and help to pay their Landlord's Rent; their Corn and Cattle being already seized, and *Money a Thing Unknown.*"

The third reason given in favor of the proposal is that a new dish will be introduced to the tables of "all *Gentlemen of Fortune* in the Kingdom, who have any Refinement of Taste. . . ." The fifth reason is that the trade of "Houses frequented by all the *fine Gentlemen*, who justly value themselves upon their Knowledge in good Eating" will be greatly/32/increased, especially in houses where there is a "skilful Cook, who understands how to oblige his Guests" and who "will contrive to make it as expensive as they please."

Omitting it in the next paragraph, Swift returns to the idea in the following one (27), as he visualizes the new food at all fine tables, at the Lord Mayor's feast, and (in paragraph 28) at all *"merry Meetings"* such as *"Weddings and Christenings."* (It is appropriate to the subject matter that he should single out these two occasions as examples of merry meetings.)

In the next paragraph (29) come the "Expedients" which the projector rejects. The landlords are implied in several of them, and near the end of the series are singled out: *"Of teaching Landlords to have, at least, one Degree of Mercy towards their Tenants."* In the peroration the landlords are hit two more times. They are blamed for much of the "perpetual Scene of Misfortunes," since tenants are borne down upon by "the *Oppression of Landlords. . . .*" And in the final paragraph in the recapitulation the landlords are given the strong final position in that series: *"and giving some pleasure to the Rich."*

Isolating all of these examples tends to give the impression that Swift's amazingly frequent repetition of this idea is not "refining" but merely gross pounding at a theme. However, as each instance appears in full context, Swift's subtlety is fully appreciated. Swift's refining is a rhetorical device contributing to the reader's acceptance of the irony, because its operation is pervasive, it works by indirection and by implication, it is manipulated through a careful handling of the language of each sentence, and because, when it appears, the reader's attention is frequently fixed elsewhere (on the idea of the sentence rather than on the method of the sentence).

Less Frequently Used Devices

Among less frequently used, but no less important, rhetorical devices of the "Modest Proposal" is appeal to authority. In the exordium the projector assumes that all agree as to the state of the kingdom: "I THINK that it is agreed by all Parties, that this prodigious Number of Children in the Arms, or on the Backs, or at the *Heels* of their *Mothers,* and frequently their *Fathers,* is *in the present deplorable State of the*/33/*Kingdom,* a very great additional Grievance. . . ." This appeal is of particular importance to Swift's English readers, for (as indicated in his "A Short View of the State of Ireland") many Englishmen, who were well entertained in fine houses during brief visits to Ireland, actually thought that Ireland was a prosperous kingdom and reported so back home.

"A principal Gentleman in the County of *Cavan*" has informed the projector that even in that county, which is famous for its thieves, there were not known to that gentleman over one or two instances in which children under the age of six were very skillful at stealing.

The projector has consulted the merchants, men who really should know about market prices, etc., in order to confirm his calculations, and he has been "assured by our Merchants" that children around the age of twelve are "no saleable Commodity."

Probably the most impressive single authority which the projector calls upon is that "grave" French author and physician, Rabelais, who has proved that a fish diet greatly contributes to potency in engendering this new commodity.

In addition to these explicit appeals to authority there are several implicit appeals. Each time that the projector says that certain gentlemen would pay this or that for various parts of this animal, or that such and such can be done to this commodity to please the gentlemen of fashion, he is presupposing the approval of these gentlemen. In fact one such gentleman—"a VERY worthy person, *a true Lover of his Country*" becomes so enthusiastic about the projector's plan that he "was pleased . . . to offer a Refinement on my Scheme." The older

youths could be used as a substitute for venison. But the moderation
of Swift's projector finds this suggestion excessive. Besides, "a very
knowing American" has assured the projector that such meat is tough.

The implicit approval of authority is reflected in the following remarks which are scattered at random through the essay. "No Gentleman would repine to give Ten Shillings for the *Carcase of a good fat
Child*." The flayed carcass would make admirable gloves and summer
boots. The landlords will have excellent nutritive meat "when he hath
some particular Friend, or his own Family, to dine with him." Such
meat/34/would make a "considerable Figure" at a Lord Mayor's feast.
These and the several other food passages in the essay completely
presuppose participation in and approval of the scheme by the people
of quality.

The explicit appeals to authority, especially to experts and grave
authors, are standard in classical rhetoric. The indirect and implied
approvals just enumerated, however, contribute more to the ironic
trap than do the explicit ones, for the former imply a general accep-
tation among society. Appeal to the authority of the whole society is
what Aristotle calls the appeal to "previous judgment," to a "necessary truth." If the truth is not necessary, then it can be an appeal to
"the opinion held by the majority, or the wise, or all or most of the
good."[12]

The device of interrogation is employed once in the essay. It is in
the powerful thirty-second paragraph. This paragraph opens with the
quite mild concession that the projector is "not so violently bent"
upon his own opinion that he will not entertain other proposals. He
merely makes one reservation: that any such projectors answer two
questions:

First, As Things now stand, how they will find Food and Raiment,
for a Hundred Thousand useless Mouths and Backs? And *secondly,* There being a round Million of Creatures in human Figure,
throughout this Kingdom; whose whole Subsistence, put into a
common Stock, would leave them in Debt two Millions of Pounds
Sterling; adding those, who are Beggars by Profession, to the Bulk
of Farmers, Cottagers, and Labourers, with their Wives and Children, who are Beggars in Effect; I desire those Politicians, who
dislike my Overture, and may perhaps be so bold to attempt an
Answer, that they first ask the Parents of these Mortals, Whether
they would not, at this Day, think it a great Happiness to have
been sold for Food at a Year old, in the Manner I prescribe; and

---

[12] Aristotle *Rhet.* II.xxiii.12. See also Quintilian *Instit.* V.xi.36-37.

thereby have avoided such a perpetual Scene of Misfortunes, as they have gone through; by the *Oppression of Landlords*; the Impossibility of paying Rent, without Money or Trade; the Want of common Sustenance, with neither House nor Cloaths, to cover them from the Inclemencies of Weather; and the most inevitable Prospect of entailing the like, or greater Miseries upon their Breed forever.

The final phrase "upon their Breed forever" has the inverted/35/ ring of the finality of a prayer "world without end, amen." This rhetorical question serves several purposes. It summarizes the complaints which have been scattered throughout the essay (the quotation is from the peroration) ; it is so couched that what has been given in mass would have to be refuted separately (a device which Quintilian recommends when a pleader has massed together what cannot be strong separately) ; and of course it gives the projector occasion to voice his most stinging indictment without seeming to propound, since he is merely posing a question as the basis for a possible concession on his part.

Argument by elimination is scarcely used in this essay, and in the passages in which it appears it does not occur in its full syllogistic form. It is a telling means of persuasion because it narrows the argument by excluding any consideration except the one being urged.

The passage just quoted from paragraph thirty-two is a good example of elimination, for if either question can reasonably be answered, the projector has already promised that he is ready to concede and entertain other proposals. And in paragraph nineteen in reference to the problem of old people, the projector eliminates all other problems except the one of his proposal, thus sharpening the focus on his own proposal and making the audience more ready to attack this problem with this solution, since this proposal will relieve the whole economic situation and all members of the society.

Swift uses the device of accumulation to good effect in two instances, one of which has just been quoted from paragraph thirty-two. The second question posed there is a long series which accurately and adequately summarizes the whole situation of Ireland and the modest proposal being made.

The other use of accumulation is the brief description in the final paragraph: "having no other motive than the *Publick Good of my Country, by advancing our Trade, providing for Infants, relieving the Poor, and giving some Pleasure to the Rich.*" This series concisely echoes each of the major groups of reasons which have been set forth (except the antipapist reasons, which might, from the point of view of the projector, be included "in the public Good"). It is natural that both instances of accumulation in this essay should occur in the/36/ peroration, for recapitulation is one of the standard uses of this section of the speech.

From the understatement of the essay's title forward, litotes has an unusually strong force, since it operates within the ironic inversion. Statements which would be quite ordinary understatement are surcharged by the ironically inverted context. In paragraph twelve the projector grants that this new "Food will be somewhat dear." In an essay which is *not* built upon irony of inversion, litotes operates merely to indicate more force by couching an idea in a less forceful manner than is appropriate. But to say that this food "will be somewhat dear" lifts the ironic veil in order to state a terrible truth. And the statement comes through in all its truth, with only the one word "somewhat" holding the thin thread of irony as the observation darts for the moment to the very edge of the fine line between irony and simple truth.

The same effect is achieved in paragraph seventeen. (The reference is to the gentleman's suggestion that young boys and girls could be used as a substitute for venison.) :

> And besides it is not improbable, that some scrupulous People might be apt to censure such a Practice (although indeed very unjustly) as a little bordering upon Cruelty; which, I confess, hath always been with me the strongest Objection against any Project, how well soever intended.

The single phrase "a little bordering on" holds the ironic structure tightly together during the moment that the ironist, brushing aside all except a single thin layer of irony, allows his reader a glimpse into the heart of the matter, which is that any mere proposal is cruelly fruitless since only a thoroughly normal and healthy administration of the kingdom can give genuine well-being to Ireland.

In the list of rejected "expedients" the litotes has the same function. Two of the expedients are expressed in litotes: *"Of being a little cautious not to sell our Country and Consciences for nothing: Of teaching Landlords to have, at least, one Degree of Mercy towards their Tenants."* The litotes is strong just in these isolated examples. But, when they are set into ironic inversion, they gain added power: Let no man talk to me of being a little cautious not to sell our country and consciences for nothing; let no man talk to me of teaching land-/37/lords to have, at least, one degree of mercy toward their tenants.

The negative of "Let no man talk to me" further emphasizes the already negative litotes of the *of* phrases.

Although the passage listing the expedients is not cast as a whole into litotes, the effect of the whole is quite similar to that which I have just described in connection with litotes: the ironist momentarily holds aside all but one of the several curtains of irony so that his reader may be shown the truth.

> Therefore, let no man talk to me of other Expedients: Of taxing our Absentees at five Shillings a Pound; Of using neither Cloaths, nor Household Furniture except what is of our own Growth and Manufacture: Of utterly rejecting the Materials and Instruments that promote foreign Luxury: Of curing the Expensiveness of Pride, Vanity, Idleness, and Gaming in our Women: Of introducing a Vein of Parsimony, Prudence and Temperance: Of learning to love our Country, wherein we differ even from LAPLANDERS, and the Inhabitants of TOPINAMBOO: Of quitting our Animosities, and Factions; nor act any longer like the JEWS, who were murdering one another at the very Moment their City was taken: Of being a little cautious not to sell our Country and Consciences for nothing: Of teaching Landlords to have, at least, one Degree of Mercy towards their Tenants. Lastly, Of putting a Spirit of Honesty, Industry, and Skill into our Shopkeepers; who, if a Resolution could now be taken to buy only our native Goods, would immediately unite to cheat and exact upon us in the Price, the Measure, and the Goodness; nor could ever yet be brought to make one fair Proposal of just Dealing, though often and earnestly invited to it.

Swift has left no doubt as to his real meaning: this is the only extended passage in the essay which is italicized; it is the only extended passage built upon the principle of understatement. The use of litotes is heavily limited in this essay (occurring only in the passages which have just been discussed) because the rhetoric is geared to the irony: litotes is the device which allows the ironist the thinnest facade of pretense, and obviously Swift could not allow his ironic pose to become fragile at too many points.

The projector makes several appeals directly to the emotions of his audience. One such appeal is to his reader's prejudice against Roman Catholics. Three separate passages contain this appeal. In the first paragraph of the essay such an/38/appeal is prepared for. The "helpless infants" of these starving parents will, when they grow up, become thieves, "or leave their *dear Native Country, to fight for the*

Pretender in Spain, or sell themselves to the *Barbadoes.*" The next passage is in paragraph thirteen. The projector has been assured that

> . . . *Fish being a prolifick Dyet,* there are more Children born in *Roman Catholick Countries* about Nine Months after *Lent,* than at any other Season: Therefore reckoning a Year after *Lent,* the Markets will be more glutted than usual; because the Number of *Popish Infants,* is, at least, three to one in this King-dom; and therefore it will have one other Collateral Advantage, by lessening the Number of *Papists* among us.

The subject is mentioned once more; it has the lead position in the reasons of the proof:

> For, *First,* as I have already observed, it would greatly lessen the *Number of Papists,* with whom we are yearly over-run; being the principal Breeders of the Nation, as well as our most danger-ous Enemies; and who stay at home on Purpose, with a Design to *deliver the Kingdom to the Pretender;* hoping to take their Advantage by the Absence of *so many good Protestants,* who have chosen rather to leave their Country, than stay at home, and pay Tithes against their Conscience, to an idolatrous *Epis-copal Curate.*

Stigmatizing the Roman Catholics as traitors and scolding the Anglo-Irish for not staying home and for not supporting the Established Church play right to the opinion of the Anglo-Irish. Swift's making this particular appeal raises the old and unanswerable question of whether he directed his Irish tracts to the whole of Ireland or to the Anglo-Irish minority.[13] If it is to all Irishmen, this device is hardly a happy choice.

---

[13] Quintana suggests that Swift was strongly Anglo-Irish instead of Irish (Quin-tana, *op. cit.,* pp. 246-47). Murry believes that Swift's motives are too unclear or mixed for us to determine. John Middleton Murry, *Jonathan Swift: A Critical Biography* (London: Jonathan Cape, 1954), p. 359. Davis, in his Introduction to Vol. X of his edition of *The Drapier Letters* calls attention to the fact that the Drapier addressed himself to the "whole State of Ireland" (p. xxxi). Carl Van Doren suggests that Swift's strong pro-Anglo-Irish sentiment gradually gave way to a pan-Irish sympathy by the end of the Wood campaign. Van Doren cites Swift's own comment in a letter to Pope: "I do profess without affectation, that your kind opinion of me as a patriot, since you call it so, is what I do not deserve; because what I do is owing to perfect rage and resentment, and the mortifying sight of slavery, folly, and baseness about me, among which I am forced to live." Carl Van Doren, *Swift* (New York: The Viking Press, 1930), pp. 170-71. Swift himself could probably not have determined whether his vexation against English injustice to Ireland was greater or less than his disgust at Irish apathy which accepted English policies.

The projector, with a sure knowledge of his readers' prejudice, appeals to their prejudice against dishonest shopkeepers. His appeal has a position in the long, italicized catalogue of rejected "expedients":

> Lastly, Of putting a Spirit of Honesty, Industry, and Skill into our Shop-keepers; who, if a Resolution could now be taken to buy only our native Goods, would immediately unite to cheat and exact upon us in the Price, the Measure, and the Goodness; nor could ever yet be brought to make one fair Proposal of just Dealing, though often and earnestly invited to it./39/

The statement comes with all the more force and conviction, for Swift had so often and earnestly invited them to it. This appeal works equally well to the general prejudice against shop-keepers or to the Anglo-Irish prejudice against Irish shop-keepers (in the event that the essay was directed mainly to the Anglo-Irish).

A favorite device of rhetorical appeal to the emotions is that of the "vivid picture" or, as it is sometimes called, "ocular demonstration."[14] Vividness being a standard quality in the best work of Swift, it might seem a bit beside the point to single out particular instances of this quality here. The rhetorical device is, however, usually meant to name an extended set piece of description. In addition to the general quality of vividness throughout Swift's essay, there is one of these set pieces: the opening paragraph. In this first paragraph of the exordium Swift sketches in minute detail the picture of the wandering, begging mothers and children. The device becomes even more obvious when we consider that in an essay to *prove* the validity of a proposal, the essay begins, not with a statement of the proposal, not with any preliminary arguments for the proposal, but with an actual picture of what has brought about the need for the proposal. In this sense the opening paragraph is an ocular demonstration. This is the only set picture in the essay; other passages which describe a situation tend to do so in terms too abstract or in a point of view too generalized and abstracted to give such a set picture. There are little phrases which, however, through the sure touch of the poet, give glances at little pictures, such as the final clause in this sentence: "We should soon see an honest Emulation among the married women, *which of them could bring the fattest Child to the Market.*" The last clause gives us a scene of proud and bragging mothers elbowing and vying with each other at the market place. However, such little touches tend to be more a matter of style than of rhetorical device.

---

[14] *Ad Herennium* LV.

Swift's use of parenthesis in the essay functions in four ways: two are used to introduce allusions which enrich the argument by suggesting situations never stated or explained; three are used to slip in cutting asides reflecting the judgment of the projector; one is used in connection with diminution; and another is used in balance with litotes./40/

The two which allude to arguments not specifically raised in the essay are the following: the projector points out that there is no opportunity for the employment of laborers in handicraft and agriculture: "We neither build Houses, (I mean in the Country) nor cultivate Land." The parenthesis clarifies the point. The projector does not mean primarily that construction jobs are lacking; he means that no great plantation houses are being built and that therefore there are no agricultural jobs being created. The other parenthesis of this kind is on the same subject: Dublin alone would "take off, annually, about Twenty Thousand Carcasses; and the rest of the Kingdom (where probably they will be sold somewhat cheaper) the remaining Eighty Thousand." The parenthesis again emphasizes the unfruitful conditions in the country areas. He has told his readers of the terrible conditions in Dublin, and through these two parentheses he leaves it to the reader to imagine the situation in the country, a situation even worse than that in Dublin.[15] The wealth of argument which the projector enjoys is so vast that only through these two parentheses does he have space even to indicate some lines of proof for his proposal. This is one of the most subtle refinements Swift has given to a standard rhetorical device.

In three instances Swift uses parenthesis in its more usual function of inserting an aside to his audience: "THOSE who are more thrifty (*as I must confess the Times require*) may flay the Carcase. . . ." He accomplishes little here with the parenthesis because his use of italics emphasizes what the parenthesis is supposed to tuck in unobtrusively.[16] In a similar instance, the same device has much more power because italics are used for only one word and because the remark is so cutting: this proposal will insure a more humane treatment of wives by husbands, who will no longer "offer to beat or kick them, (as is too *frequent* a Practice) for fear of a Miscarriage." "There is

---

[15] See Swift's "A Short View of the State of Ireland" for a description of the plight of the agricultural worker and of the depleted condition of many of the old plantations.

[16] In general in this essay italics are used for emphasis and might therefore be construed as a hint concerning that part of oratory called delivery. However, the well-known problems of Swift and his printers on such textual matters render only dubious authenticity to any particular italics. We cannot know for sure whether some are Swift's or his printer's.

likewise another Advantage in my *Scheme*, that it will prevent those *voluntary Abortions*, and that horrid Practice of *Women murdering their Bastard Children*; alas! too frequent among us; sacrificing their *poor innocent Babes. . . .*"

Two occasions of Swift's use of parenthesis are crucial to the passages in which they occur. Both have been discussed/41/above, in connection with litotes and diminution, respectively. As has been noticed above, the projector has been careful gradually to refine *beggar* so that it will include all of the poor of Ireland. At the delicate point where the identification is completely made, parenthesis is brought into play to perform this task: "I HAVE already computed the Charge of nursing a Beggar's Child (in which list I reckon all *Cottagers, Labourers,* and Four fifths of the *Farmers*). . . ."

As we have seen, too, the passages in the essay where Swift employs litotes become thin in respect to the degree of irony present. In one such instance Swift uses parenthesis to help balance the litotes: some people "might be apt to censure such a Practice (although indeed very unjustly) as a little bordering on Cruelty. . . ." Since only the litotes keeps this statement from being a literal expression of the simple truth, the ironical negation of the parenthesis helps balance the litotes and thus helps to maintain the irony.

Conclusions

"A Modest Proposal" is a brilliant example of the use of non-argumentative devices of rhetorical persuasion. The whole essay, of course, rests broadly upon argument of cause and effect: these causes have produced this situation in Ireland, and this proposal will result in these effects in Ireland. But Swift, within the general framework of this argument, does not employ specific argumentative forms in this essay. The projector chooses rather to *assert* his reasons and then to amass them by way of proof. He does not argue his reasons, and he does not prove them with formal arguments. In introducing the proof, the projector states that "I think the Advantages by the Proposal which I have made, are obvious, and many, as well as of the highest Importance." The fact that his reasons are "obvious" indicates that they need not be proved by argument. After having listed the sixth reason, he states that many more advantages could be "enumerated." This last word indicates that he is making no effort to prove, but merely to list. This refusal to argue his reasons is of course a persuasive device in itself, for it places the whole proposal upon the plane of obvious fact, necessary truth, rather than upon the plane of argued postulates open to debate./42/

Although the essay is not logically complex, it is extremely complex rhetorically—as is easily seen, for example, by the number of times in the preceding pages that a single passage has been used to demonstrate several devices which are operating at once.

Swift's ironic norm is established by the pervasive tone of diminution (human beings to animals) and by the projector's sustained point of view as an economist (his mathematics, his dealing with people as only statistical abstractions, his assuming that everyone will participate in this new industry). The human flesh is so consistently regarded as just another commodity that the whole society is finally drawn into a participation in the project—the producers, the sellers, and the consumers. This complete involvement of all classes of citizens into the scheme is arrived at by the subtle use of rhetorical devices which we have been examining—especially by the processes of diminution (for the producers) and refining (for the consumers). The norm is so thoroughly established that if the reader demurs, he will find himself to be the only one out of step.

In addition to the extensive use of these two devices of classical rhetoric, there is the fundamental ethical proof which informs the whole essay. Swift has fully exploited the possibilities of this proof by his thorough development of the character of the projector, whose personality is evident either implicitly or explicitly in every paragraph of the essay. And within these elaborately employed devices are manipulated the rhetorical devices which Swift uses less often: his direct and implied authorities; his appeal to the emotions through ocular demonstration and through the prejudices of the Irish and the Anglo-Irish; his rhetorical interrogation to allow him to assert strongly while he seems only to question mildly; his use of elimination, whereby all other proposals except his are swept aside; his uncanny use of litotes to hold the ironic pose by a single fine wire while truth is allowed to peek through for a moment; his effortless use of parenthesis to indicate whole areas of reasons which have had to be crowded out of the main line of proof; his repeatedly implied refusal to argue the "obvious." By the consummate skill with which Swift has interlocked these several devices of classical rhetoric, he/43/ has created "A Modest Proposal." To appreciate how fundamental the classical rhetoric is to the very texture of the essay, one need merely ask himself what the essay would be like if Swift had not availed himself of the long tradition of such rhetoric as it reached right down to Swift's own school days. To answer that the essay simply would not exist in its present perfection would be a conservative reply.

Appendix

The Answer to the *Craftsman**

Sir, I detest reading your papers, because I am not of your principles, and because I cannot endure to be convinced. Yet, I was prevailed on to peruse your *Craftsman* of December the 12th, wherein I discover you to be as great an enemy of this country as you are of your own. You are pleased to reflect on a project I proposed of making the children of Irish parents to be useful to the public instead of being burdensome; and you venture to assert, that your own scheme is more charitable, of not permitting our Popish natives to be listed in the service of any foreign prince.

Perhaps, sir, you may not have heard of any kingdom so unhappy as this, both in their imports and exports. We import a sort of goods, of no intrinsic value, which costs us above forty thousand pounds a year to dress, and scour, and polish them, which altogether do not yield one penny advantage; and we annually export above seven hundred thousand pounds a year in another kind of goods, for which we receive not one single farthing in return: even the money paid for the letters sent in transacting this commerce being all returned to England. But now, when there is a most lucky opportunity offered to begin a trade, whereby this nation will save many thousand pounds a year, and England be a prodigious gainer, you are pleased, without call, officiously and maliciously to interpose with very frivolous arguments.

It is well known, that, about sixty years ago, the exportation of live cattle from hence to England was of great benefit to both kingdoms, until that branch of traffic was stopped by an Act of Parliament on your side, whereof you have had sufficient reason to repent. Upon which account, when another Act passed your Parliament, forbidding the exportation of live men to any foreign country, you were so wise to put in a clause, allowing it to be done by his Majesty's permission, under his sign manual, for which, among other great benefits granted

---

*For bibliographical information, see page 9 of this edition.

121

to Ireland, we are infinitely obliged to the British legislature. Yet this very grace and favor you, Mr. D'Anvers, whom we never disobliged, are endeavoring to prevent; which, I will take it upon me to say, is a manifest mark of your disaffection to his Majesty, a want of duty to the ministry, and a wicked design of oppressing this kingdom, and a traitorous attempt to lessen the trade and manufacture of England.

Our truest and best ally the most Christian King has obtained his Majesty's licence, pursuant to law, to export from hence some thousand bodies of healthy, young, living men, to supply his Irish regiments. The King of Spain, as you assert yourself, has desired the same civility, and seems to have at least as good a claim; supposing then that these two potentates will only desire leave to carry off six thousand men between them to France and Spain, then by computing the maintenance of a tall, hungry, Irish man, in food and clothes, to be only five pounds a head, here will be thirty thousand pounds per annum saved clear to the nation, for they can find no other employment at home beside begging, robbing, or stealing. But, if thirty, forty, or fifty thousand (which we could gladly spare) were sent on the same errand, what an immense benefit must it be to us; and, if the two princes, in whose service they were, should happen to be at war with each other, how soon would those recruits be destroyed, then what a number of friends would the Pretender lose, and what a number of Popish enemies all true protestants get rid of. Add to this, that then by such a practice, the lands of Ireland that want hands for tillage, must be employed in grazing, which would sink the price of wool, raw hides, butter, and tallow, so that the English might have them at their own rates; and in return send us wheat to make our bread, barley to brew our drink, and oats for our horses, without any labor of our own.

Upon this occasion, I desire humbly to offer a scheme, which, in my opinion, would best answer the true interests of both kingdoms: for, although I bear a most tender, filial affection to England, my dear, native country; yet, I cannot deny but this noble island has a great share in my love and esteem, nor can I express how much I desire to see it flourish in trade and opulence, even beyond its present happy condition.

The profitable land of this kingdom is, I think, usually computed at seventeen millions of acres, all which I propose to be wholly turned to grazing. Now, it is found by experience that, one grazier and his family can manage two thousand acres. Thus, sixteen millions eight hundred thousand acres may be managed by eight thousand four hundred families, and the fraction of two hundred thousand acres will be more than sufficient for cabins, out-houses, and potato gardens; because, it is to be understood, that corn of all sorts must be sent to us from England.

These eight thousand four hundred families may be divided among the four provinces, according to the number of houses in each province; and, making the equal allowance of eight to a family, the number of inhabitants will amount to sixty seven thousand two hundred souls; to these we are to add a standing army of twenty thousand English, which, together with their trulls, their bastards, and their horse-boys, will, by a gross computation, very near double the count, and be very sufficient for the defence and grazing of the kingdom, as well as to enrich our neighbors, expel Popery, and keep out the Pretender. And lest the army should be at a loss for business, I think it would be very prudent to employ them in collecting the public taxes for paying themselves and the civil list.

I advise, that all the owners of these lands should live constantly in England, in order to learn politeness, and qualify themselves for employments: but, for fear of increasing the natives in this island, that an annual draft, according to the number born every year, be exported to whatever prince will bear the carriage; or transplanted to the English dominions on the American continent, as a screen between his Majesty's English subjects and the savage Indians.

I advise likewise, that no commodity whatsoever, of this nation's growth, should be sent to any other country, except England, under the penalty of high treason; and that all said commodities shall be sent in their natural state, the hides raw, the wool uncombed, the flax in the stub; excepting only fish, butter, tallow and whatever else will be spoiled in the carriage. On the contrary, that no goods whatsoever shall be imported hither, except from England, under the same penalty: that England should be forced, at their own rates, to send us over clothes ready made, as well as shirts and smocks to the soldiers and their trulls; all iron, wooden, and earthen ware; and whatever furniture may be necessary for the cabins of graziers, with a sufficient quantity of gin, and other spirits, for those who can afford to get drunk of holydays.

As to the civil and ecclesiastical administration, which I have not yet fully considered, I can say little; only with regard to the latter, it is plain, that the article of paying tythe for supporting speculative opinions in religion, which is so insupportable a burden to all true protestants, and to most Churchmen, will be very much lessened by this expedient; because dry cattle pay nothing to the spiritual hireling, any more than imported corn; so that the industrious shepherd and cow-herd may sit, every man under his own blackberry bush, and on his own potato bed, whereby this happy island will become a new Arcadia.

I do likewise propose that no money shall be used in Ireland, except what is made of leather, which likewise shall be coined in England, and imported, and that the taxes shall be levied out of the commodities we export to England, and there turned into money for his Majesty's use; and the rents to landlords discharged in the same manner. This will be no manner of grievance; for we already see it very practicable to live without money, and shall be more convinced of it every day. But whether paper shall still continue to supply that defect, or whether we shall hang up all those who profess the trade of bankers, (which latter I am rather inclined to) must be left to the consideration of wiser politicians.

That which makes me more zealously bent upon this scheme, is my desire of living in amity with our neighboring brethren; for we have already tried all other means, without effect, to that blessed end: and, by the course of measures taken for some years past, it should seem that we are all agreed to the point.

This expedient will be of great advantage to both kingdoms, upon several accounts: for, as to England, they have a just claim to the balance of trade on their side with the whole world; and therefore our ancestors and we, who conquered this kingdom for them, ought, in duty and gratitude, to let them have the whole benefit of that conquest to themselves; especially when the conquest was amicably made, without bloodshed, by a stipulation between the Irish princes and Henry II by which they paid him, indeed, not equal homage with what the Electors of Germany do to the emperor, but very near the same that he did to the King of France for his French dominions.

In consequence of this claim from England, that kingdom may very reasonably demand the benefit of all our commodities in their natural growth, to be manufactured by their people, and a sufficient quantity of them for our use to be returned hither fully manufactured.

This, on the other side, will be of great benefit to our inhabitants the graziers, when time and labor will be too much taken up in manuring their ground, feeding their cattle, shearing their sheep, and sending over their oxen fit for slaughter; to which employments they are turned by nature, as descended from the Scythians, whose diet they are still so fond of. So Virgil describes it:

> *Et lac concretum cum sanguine bibit equino.*

Which, in English, is bonnyclabber, mingled with the blood of horses, as they formerly did, until about the beginning of the last century, luxury, under the form of politeness, began to creep in, they changed the blood of horses for that of their black cattle; and, by consequence, became less warlike than their ancestors.

Although I proposed that the army should be collectors of the public revenues, yet I did not thereby intend those taxes should be paid in gold or silver, but in kind, as all other rent: for the custom of tenants making their payments in money, is a new thing in the world, little known in former ages, nor generally practiced in any nation at present, except this island and the southern parts of Britain. But, to my great satisfaction, I foresee better times; the ancient manner begins to be practiced in many parts of Connaught, as well as in the County of Corke, where the 'Squires turn tenants to themselves, divide so many cattle to their slaves, who are to provide such a quantity of butter, hides, or tallow, still keeping up their number of cattle; and carry the goods to Corke, or other port towns, and then sell them to the merchants. By which invention there is no such thing as a ruined farmer to be seen; but the people live with comfort on potatoes and bonnyclabber, neither of which are vendible commodities abroad.

Suggestions for Papers

Short Papers

Murry has said that there is none of the usual light-hearted Swiftian humor in "A Modest Proposal." Show that even within this dire proposal there is still playful humor.

Swift was an inveterate punster. Isolate the puns in "A Modest Proposal" and try to establish what effect such punning has on the essay.

Choose one of these critical articles and explain how you think it to be the least relevant to your understanding of "A Modest Proposal."

Does either essay by Swift have satiric techniques not found in the other? Explain, and if you can, account for their absence.

Some critics have argued that the whole concept of the *persona* is faulty and that one should read Swift's ironic essays believing that the voice is always Swift's. What do you think? Formulate your own thesis on this question and defend it by an analysis of one or both of Swift's essays.

Swift has been praised for his ability to maintain the smooth ironic surface of "A Modest Proposal." Consider this aspect of his essay and explain it, with examples from the essay. Does Swift ever slip?

If you accept the contention that the voice of the Modest Proposer is directly his and indirectly Swift's, isolate those elements of prose style which you think are present in the essay mainly to contribute to Swift's characterization of his fictive author.

Swift is a master of the innuendo. Analyze a number of the more "loaded" sentences of "A Modest Proposal" and show how Swift is often able to insinuate or imply ideas which he never actually states in a matter-of-fact way.

As noted in the Introduction, a satire of negative irony often leaves the reader somewhat at a loss to know exactly what the satirist is in favor of. Make as many positive statements as you can deduce from your reading of both of Swift's essays in order to compile a series of generalizations stating what Swift favored.

Neo-classical writers such as Swift are reputed to be quite good at keeping their distance from both their subject and their reader, as opposed to Romantic writers, who are more likely to expose their own egos as they write. Analyze "A Modest Proposal" to show how Swift gains this objectivity and maintains real or apparent distancing.

After a careful study of "A Modest Proposal" you should be able to write an essay on "What Is Irony and How Does It Work?" Using examples from both of Swift's essays, see whether you can now articulate your own concept of irony and its operation.

Long Papers

Analyze the vocabulary of the Modest Proposer in an effort to determine how it contributes to the satire of the essay.

Choose two or three of these critical articles and explain how you think them to be the most relevant of this collection in aiding you more keenly to comprehend "A Modest Proposal."

Choose one or two of these critical articles and explain how you think them to be the least relevant to a study of "A Modest Proposal."

Isolate four major Swiftian techniques of satire in "A Modest Proposal" and show, with examples from Swift's text, how they operate in the essay.

Having determined the techniques mentioned in the topic above, show how they operate in or are absent from "An Answer to the *Craftsman.*"

Determine and explain with examples as many different satiric techniques as you can which Swift uses in "A Modest Proposal."

Follow directions for the topic above for "An Answer to the *Craftsman.*"

Does Swift fail or succeed in his effort to make "An Answer to the *Craftsman*" seem to be written by the Modest Proposer? Justify your answer with examples from Swift's two essays.

The basic system of punctuation Swift uses for "A Modest Proposal" is quite different from that of "An Answer to the *Craftsman*." Find the differences between the two and try to account for them.

Daniel Defoe, a contemporary of Swift, wrote an ironic essay "The Shortest Way with Dissenters," in which he ironically argued that killing the dissenters was the only way that the Established Church of England and the English government could solve the problem of these unorthodox Christian groups. Read Defoe's essay and then write an essay in which you contrast the satiric techniques used by these two writers showing which essay is the more successful satire.

Swift is generally praised for the conciseness of his prose style, for the fact that, like a poet, he can say and imply more in fewer words than most writers of prose. Assuming that the conciseness of the style of "A Modest Proposal" is entirely Swift's (and not the Modest Proposer's), examine this aspect of "A Modest Proposal" and show how this thesis is substantially true.

If, after repeated readings and study, you find "A Modest Proposal" highly overrated as a great satire, write an essay in which you attack its reputation and give your counter arguments.

Select a twentieth-century satire (a movie, a novel, or a play) which you know and like a great deal and compare it to "A Modest Proposal" for technique, power, and underlying value system of the satirist.

Imitation is often a good way to demonstrate that you comprehend a literary work. Choose a situation which you know about which needs exposing and correcting and write your own Modest Proposal, after the manner of Swift.

Additional Readings

Bullitt, John M. *Jonathan Swift and the Anatomy of Satire: A Study of Satiric Technique.* Cambridge: Harvard University Press, 1953.

Davis, Herbert. "The Conciseness of Swift," in *Essays on the Eighteenth Century Presented to David Nichol Smith.* Oxford: The Clarendon Press, 1945.

————. *The Satire of Jonathan Swift.* New York: Macmillan, 1947.

Dobrée, Bonamy. *English Literature in the Early Eighteenth Century.* Oxford: The Clarendon Press, 1959.

Ehrenpreis, Irvin. "Personae," in *Restoration and Eighteenth Century Literature: Essays in Honor of Alan Dugald McKillop.* Ed. Carroll Camden. Chicago: The University of Chicago Press, 1963.

————. *Swift: The Man, His Works, and the Age.* London: Methuen. Vols. I and II now published, 1962, 1968.

FitzGerald, Brian. *The Anglo-Irish, Three Representative Types: Corke, Ormonde, Swift.* New York: Staples Press, 1952.

Fussell, Paul Jr. *The Rhetorical World of Augustan Humanism: Ethics and Imagery from Swift to Burke.* Oxford: The Clarendon Press, 1965.

Holloway, John. "The Well-filled Dish: An Analysis of Swift's Satire," *The Hudson Review,* IX (Spring, 1956), 20-37.

Kernan, Alvin B. *The Plot of Satire.* New Haven: Yale University Press, 1965.

Knox, Norman. *The Word "Irony" and Its Contexts,* 1500-1755. Durham: Duke University Press, 1961.

Landa, Louis A. "Swift's Economic Views and Mercantilism," *English Literary History,* X (December, 1943), 310-335.

———— and James Edward Tobin. *Jonathan Swift: A List of Critical Studies Published from 1895 to 1945.* New York: Cosmopolitan Science and Art Service Company, 1945.

Leavis, F. R. "The Irony of Swift," *Scrutiny,* II (March, 1934), 364-378. Reprinted in *The Common Pursuit.* London: Chatto and Windus, 1952.

Lecky, William Edward Hartpole. *A History of Ireland in the Eighteenth Century.* 5 Volumes. New York: D. Appleton and Company, 1893.

Maxwell, Constantia. *Dublin under the Georges, 1714-1830.* London: Faber and Faber, 1956 (Revised Edition).

Murry, John Middleton. *Jonathan Swift: A Critical Biography.* London: Jonathan Cape, 1954; and New York: Noonday Press, 1955.

Price, Martin. *To the Palace of Wisdom.* Garden City, New York: Doubleday, 1964, pp. 179-218.

Ross, John F. *Swift and Defoe: A Study in Relationship.* Berkeley: University of California Press, 1941.

Smith, Charles Kay. "Toward a 'Participatory Rhetoric': Teaching Swift's *Modest Proposal,*" *College English,* XXX (November, 1968), 135-149.

Stathis, James J. *A Bibliography of Swift Studies 1945-1965.* Nashville: Vanderbilt University Press, 1967.

Swift, Jonathan. *The Prose Writings of Jonathan Swift,* Herbert Davis, General Editor, 14 Volumes. Oxford: Blackwell, 1939-1968.

_____. *The Correspondence of Jonathan Swift.* Ed. Sir Harold Williams. 3 Volumes. Oxford: The Clarendon Press, 1963-1965.

Watkins, W. B. C. *Perilous Balance: The Tragic Genius of Swift, Johnson, and Sterne.* Cambridge, Mass.: Walker-de Berry, 1960.

Wittkowsky, George. "Swift's *Modest Proposal:* The Biography of an Early Georgian Pamphlet," *A Journal of the History of Ideas,* IV (January, 1943), 75-104.

Worcester, David. *The Art of Satire.* Cambridge: Harvard University Press, 1940.